THE STORY OF OXFORD

THE STORY OF
OXFORD

S. P. B. MAIS

Photography by
LEONARD AND MARJORIE GAYTON

STAPLES PRESS

STAPLES PRESS LIMITED STAPLES PRESS INCORPORATED
Mandeville Place, London *70 East 45th Street, New York*

FIRST PUBLISHED 1951

COPYRIGHT RESERVED

This Book is set in 11 on 12 point 'Monotype' Baskerville series

Made and printed in England by
STAPLES PRINTERS LIMITED
at their Kettering, Northants, establishment

Contents

Illustrations

Preface

What does he know of Oxford who only Oxford knows?

During my four years in residence as a member of the House (Christ Church) between 1905 and 1909 I certainly did not realize that I was living in a Golden Age or that the time would come when I should see the Colleges that face the 'High' shaken to their foundations by a never-ending stream of heavy lorries, tanks, motor cars and buses that threaten destruction not only to some of the fairest buildings in Europe but also to any foolhardy adventurer who seeks to cross the road.

I did not dream in those far-off days that I should live to see the day when I should have to put up a last desperate fight against the City Council to preserve the only remaining open green space in the long length of the tree-fringed Woodstock Road from being occupied by a Primary School.

Perhaps it is only those of us who have returned to our first love after long absence who realize how severe have been the changes in the last forty-five years and cherish in consequence the more dearly what remains.

It is only now after long absence and much restless travelling over the world that I am beginning to discover a few of her secrets, a little of the enchantment that none can utter.

If you are wise you will avoid Cornmarket Street which is indistinguishable from High Street, Tooting.

If you are wise you will shut your eyes, if you can, to quite half this sadly ravaged city, but in spite of what is so oddly called progress you will still find some reminders of Oxford's ancient glory if you walk warily.

I can't do more than lift the curtain here and there and point to a few of the treasures that are still to be admired. Oxford has to be discovered by each traveller for himself.

There is still thirteenth century stained glass in the windows of Merton, which also boasts the oldest, though not the largest, library (1373).

There are still 'old masters' in Christ Church, Worcester and St John's, and in the Ashmolean the finest examples of early Italian paintings outside the National Gallery.

In the Ashmolean, too, is a fine collection of classical sculpture, famous marbles, Greek vases, as well as King Alfred's Jewel, Powhatan's Mantle and Guy Fawkes's Lantern.

The Bodleian library is one of the great libraries of the world and among

7

its treasures you will see a First Folio Shakespeare and many relics of Shelley.

Corpus retains the finest collection of plate and the magnificent staff of Bishop Foxe.

Your main aim will be to visit the Colleges and try to discover what it was that Lewis Carroll and John Wesley found in Christ Church, Cecil Rhodes and Sir Walter Raleigh in Oriel, Lovelace and de Quincey in Worcester, Hobbes and Evelyn Waugh in Hertford, Edmund Gibbon and Oscar Wilde in Magdalen, Sir Thomas Browne and Dr Johnson in Pembroke, Shelley and Rochester in University, and Christopher Wren and Robert Blake in Wadham, that made them the men they were.

The courts (we call them 'quads') are full of shades, and it is for shades that you are looking quite as much as for high lights of architecture.

With this object in view remember that most colleges have open gates and that there is no charge. The porter at the lodge is there to help you. He is not Cerberus. He is Nestor.

Let your motto be 'Stop, Look and Listen'. *Festina lente*.

Don't rush your fences. Three colleges a day is a full meal. Four induces indigestion.

Finally, remember that the spirit of Oxford is elusive. Don't be disappointed if you fail to find it in a day.

I have been looking for it for nearly half a century, and only occasionally do I catch a glimpse of it – in Magdalen Tower seen from Christ Church Meadows under a full moon, in St John's Gardens on an afternoon in June, in . . .

But come and search for yourself.

S. P. B. M.

OXFORD, 1951

O mihi praeteritos referat si Juppiter annos.

Eheu fugaces, Postume,Postume,
Labuntur anni.

But if the while I think on thee, dear friend,
All losses are restored, and sorrows end.

B

IN OXFORD NOW

When 'mid this glory I was young
    I read my task and played my game,
Happy with ancient book and tongue,
    Warmed with the old and alien flame.

Greeks of the gleaming isles, I trod
    Your ways of wisdom, sailed your ships,
Apollo, Son of Light, my god,
    Your songs of Freedom on my lips.

None taught my dazzled eyes to view
    The homely works of native men:
The pillar-majesty I knew
    Of Pheidias, but not of Wren.

The blaze of autumn's oriflammes
    On England's miracle of stone
Was just the workshop of exams,
    Unloved, untasted, and unknown.

Now come I back, with eyes unseel'd;
    And beauty shines, where none had shone.
I slake my heart by stream and field,
    In Oxford meet my Parthenon.

I. B.
(*By kind permission of the author*)

CHAPTER I

My Opinion of Oxford:

What It Is and What It Might Be

OXFORD, always in the news, has never been so much in the news as now. With 8,000 undergraduates in residence many problems undreamt of in the Oxford of my undergraduate years, forty years ago, present themselves.

I am in the very unusual position of being back in the University to which I owed so much between the years 1905 and 1909, not in any official capacity. When I was bombed out of my Sussex home I could find nowhere else to live.

The onlooker not only sees most of the game. He is at complete liberty to criticize. Were I a member of the Hebdomadal Council I should, either because of loyalty to the University or because I was afraid of losing my job, be compelled to refrain from criticism.

When I came back to Oxford in 1940 I disliked nearly everything about it. As a public school master I dared to raise my voice against abuses from the inside. As an elderly graduate of the finest University in the world I feel entitled to say precisely what I feel about an institution to which I owe practically everything in life. 'My mother drunk or sober' has never been my motto. Like Hamlet I accuse not only myself of such things and so on, but also my mother, wife and children.

Oxford which could reasonably house about 90,000 people was suddenly called upon to house double that number. The trains to London, like the main streets, were a nightmare. There was no place to sleep, nothing in the shops to buy.

Coming back to Oxford for me was like coming back after long years to visit the girl with whom in the first flush of youth one had fallen deeply and finally in love, knowing her to be unattainable had wisely gone away, but had not ceased to dream of, comparing her with all other girls, as Doctor Faustus compared Helen of Troy with all other girls. Then had come the awakening, the discovery that this fairest of all good women had degenerated with the years into a virago, a slatternly and decrepit harlot.

Her traffic was the most dangerous, her train service the most dilatory, her climate the most unhealthy I had ever known.

I have before me a copy of an Oxford preparatory school magazine, *The Draconian*, dated August 1938 in which the then head master wrote:

'Boys, as testified by parents, thrive better at Oxford in term-time than during the holidays at home,' and adds a personal note. 'After six years at Rossall – in the much vaunted Blackpool ozone – I was by no means strong, but have become increasingly robust during subsequent life, almost entirely passed in Oxford.'

It is commonly asserted that the Oxford climate is good for young children and the very old. My own two small daughters went down with pneumonia, and so, at the age of 62, did I.

Undergraduates nearly all feel an appalling malaise or lassitude overtake them in this fog-bound, damp river valley.

The fact remains that first I and then my wife became mentally unstable. Without good health you might as well be dead. Without wealth or at any rate a living wage you might as well be dead. I had neither health nor wealth.

When I returned to Oxford I was full of energy and high spirits. Within a few months I was unable to sleep at night or to stay awake by day. When I returned to Oxford I was broadcasting regularly and writing profitably.

Within a few months I stopped writing altogether. My inspiration completely dried up. I was quietly dropped by the B.B.C.

My only income came from Radley, to which school I cycled in all weathers seven miles each day for a salary of £300 a year. The fees for my two daughters at the Dragon School came to more than that. I was fighting a losing battle physically, morally and financially. It is scarcely to be wondered at that I took a dim view of Oxford and only prayed for death.

I was living in a semi-detached villa two and a half miles from the shopping centre where my wife had to stand for hours in queues in ice and snow, fog, and rain only to be refused most of the necessities of life. It is little wonder that we both nearly collapsed under the strain.

I who had earned through the years an enviably high reputation as a public school master found myself totally unable to teach or even to arouse the interest of any boy; my wife, one of the most placid and even-tempered people whom I had ever met became unbalanced and hysterical.

The war was of course partly to blame, but in spite of the war I met other schoolmasters who had not lost their knack of teaching, other women who were sailing through life on an even keel.

I attribute my family disaster in large measure to the Oxford climate.

There is of course nothing we can do about it, except recognize in all honesty that it does not boast the best climate for a university, indeed that it shares with Cambridge the doubtful honour of being the worst climate in the British Isles.

Yet good work is being done here, and quite a large percentage of the population remain uncertifiable.

It is possible to become acclimatized. After ten years I now find that I am working better, longer and at higher speed than at any other time in my life. I am at my desk by three o'clock every morning and though I almost invariably go to sleep in the cinema or theatre at night that might happen to me anywhere.

The old prints of Oxford reveal a city so lovely that one can hardly believe that it is not the artist's dream. The new photographs reveal a shambles.

As Mr Thomas Sharp rightly reminds us in the opening words of his *Oxford Replanned*, 'There is probably no place-name in the world that carries so many emotional over-tones as the name Oxford.'

I am certainly prouder of the fact that I am an Oxford man than I am of the fact that I belong to one of the oldest and most honoured families in Great Britain. My loyalty to Oxford takes precedence to my loyalty to England just as a boy's loyalty to his house at school takes precedence to his loyalty to the school itself.

That is why I was so horrified to come back in 1940 and see what a deterioration there had been since I went down in 1909.

That Mr Sharp should share my horror was only to be expected. Oxford, as he says, is a public figure. It has a peculiar kind of aliveness that has no need of artificial cultivation. What it needs is to be safeguarded, safeguarded by a piece of surgery in its spinal column, restoring lost amenities, and rehabilitating old functions that have been compromised.

It is a highly vulnerable city both from the air, the land and water. The floods of February and March 1947 threatened to submerge and did indeed cut off many of Oxford's suburbs for an uncomfortable number of days and nights.

I have seen an air view photograph of North Oxford taken by the Germans which includes my house. The attack from the air never came.

The attack from the land by way of traffic is, in the words of Mr Sharp, 'threatening to break down the entire organization of Oxford as a centre of civilized life.' You have only to look at a road-map of England to see the reason for this. Oxford is on the main route from London to the Midlands, from London to South Wales, from North-West England to South-East England, from the North to the South.

Living as I do in the Woodstock Road I have plenty of opportunity of gauging the weight of traffic that passes through the city. The Woodstock Road, except in Spring when the lilac and laburnum and chestnut trees make even lorry drivers wax lyrical, is not a thing of beauty. The High Street is. It is one of the most lovely streets in the world. The number of people who see it is infinitesimal. Their attention is concentrated on preserving their lives.

'The whole centre of Oxford has become like an old garden in which circumstances have decreed that an Army manoeuvre must take place.'

So great is the volume of traffic that now lumbers up and down the High that the colleges that face it are in danger of falling down.

Alternative routes have been devised by many planners to divert the traffic that now threatens the safety of these colleges.

Mr Sharp's is simple, but has raised acute controversy. He wishes to substitute what he calls the Merton Mall, a wide road through Christ Church Meadows whose beauty so far has been preserved inviolate and whose acreage has been considered sacrosanct.

In spite of the fact that I am a Christ Church man I approve of Mr Sharp's plan. The chance of its being adopted seems to me to be slight.

But if Christ Church Meadows are to lose their pristine and age-old quietude there must I think be a guarantee that the High Street shall recover. No one should be permitted to drive along the High other than Members of the University and local business men and tradespeople on their lawful occasions. This could easily be brought about by the introduction of toll-gates on the east side of Magdalen Bridge and on the west side of Carfax.

If there is an excuse for the retention of the toll-gate at the bridge over the Thames at Eynsham, there is ten times more reason for the introduction of toll-gates to reduce the traffic through the High.

What is to be done about bicycles I frankly do not know. Eight thousand undergraduates have to race speedily at each hour's end from a lecture in one college to a lecture in another college which may be a thousand yards or even a mile away. Games-playing undergraduates have to reach grounds that are sometimes a mile, sometimes two miles away from their college or their digs. Without a bicycle an undergraduate's life is impossible.

The plain truth is that many of the present streets, Holywell and Merton Street, Magpie Lane and Blue Boar Lane for example are still medieval in width, and scarcely capable to taking the cycling traffic, for in addition to the undergraduates there are the workers at Cowley and at Morris radiators, nearly all of whom have to get to and from their factories on bicycles.

Even if the whole of the motor traffic were compulsorily diverted to a circular by-pass there would still be dangerous congestion.

In almost any other city the solution would be simple, but in spite of what a recent Mayor of Oxford and most 'progressive' industrialists say, the only Oxford that matters is Oxford University, and no one in his senses has yet suggested the demolition of the ancient colleges in order to widen the High. Most particularly is it necessary in this age of wholesale spoliation of the countryside and demolition of ancient and lovely places to make a desperate stand to preserve whatever is worth preserving in Oxford, and what is worth preserving is the ancient University where even in my time it was possible for Fellows of All Souls to continue a philosophic discussion as they crossed the High to Barclay's Bank.

There are, of course, cases of loveliness even in modern Oxford. The cube, the cylinder and the cone of the old Bodleian, St. Mary's Church and the Radcliffe Camera, 'each as sophisticated a piece of architecture as there is', stand in an area where no wheeled traffic passes on the west and only one-way traffic on the east, so that it is possible even for a hurrying American to experience a first-class aesthetic thrill and to gaze not only with safety but considerable awe at the pinnacles and spires that surround him. It is even possible to read in the Radcliffe and Bodleian, if you are lucky enough to get a book, without being in earshot of the bulldozers, 'Queen Marys', lorries and tanks that block Cornmarket Street and the High.

St Giles and the Broad, of course, carry a great deal of traffic but they are mercifully wide enough to take even the modern vehicles. They are beyond the bottleneck. St Giles with its high trees and high lamp standards is still, except during St Giles' Fair, a place of dignity and beauty.

If Oxford is to remain Oxford she must retain her ancient colleges and gardens, the High, the Broad, Holywell, the Turl, Ship Street, Long Wall Street, Merton Street and a good deal more intact.

But what of the interminable stretch of the two parallel roads, the Woodstock and Banbury Roads, with their

'Red brick and gables, Gothic spires, freestone and knick-knackery,
   Steep narrow stairs, dark kitchens, the greenhouse, the rockery'
erected in that spacious late Victorian era when dons were not only allowed to marry but also encouraged to raise enormous families.

Dons are still free to marry and frequently do. Economic necessity has deprived them of the right to a quiver-full of children, and the freedom to work an eight-hour day in crowded factories has robbed them of any domestic help.

The red brick villa with its spacious garden that once housed a single Tutor of St John's and his family and staff is now a rabbit-warren of flats, a colony of bowler-hatted negroes, or a hostel of hatless poor whites training to become secretaries or domestic scientists. The basements are no longer the haunt of idle servants but have been converted into the combined kitchen-nursery-sittingroom-study and bedroom of ex-service undergraduates, their overworked young wives and their infants. Some of these villas have been converted into schools, others into departments of the Admiralty and other Government offices, others into Private hotels, one into a Correspondence college, many of them house doctors and a few house dons. The wealthier dons have retired to the woods on Boar's Hill where the nightingale is still to be heard. The tradespeople content themselves with the nearer estates that sprawl over Headington and Cumnor hills.

A large number of Nuffield workers, many of them emigrants from Wales, have taken possession of what was once the village of Cowley, but is now a tolerable sized town.

But the working population of Oxford (and by working I take the term to include those who work an unlimited number of hours a day with their heads in addition to the mass who are forbidden to work more than eight hours a day with their hands) has grown so unwieldy that Witney, Wallingford, Abingdon, Wheatley, Kidlington, Eynsham, Didcot, Radley, Bickley, Islip, and dozens more once attractive villages and market towns have become dormitories for undergraduates, shop assistants and Morris employees. The result is congestion on the roads, in the buses, and most of all in the restaurants.

Oxford for its size is the worst served city in the British Isles for hotels and cafés.

In Stratford-upon-Avon there are 37.1 hotel bedrooms per thousand of the population, in Oxford only 2.3 per thousand and Oxford is expected to cater for industrialists as well as tourists which Stratford does not. The result is that it is quite hopeless to try to book a bedroom in Oxford, and next door to impossible to get a meal.

There is one extremely good restaurant, the Kemp, but that is a cafeteria and in term-time almost entirely thronged with undergraduates who cannot get sufficient food for their needs in Hall, but have as often as not to dine twice nightly to satisfy their appetites.

Oxford, in a word, is in a mess. As Mr Sharp reminds us, in the last twenty-five years Oxford has doubled its size; new schools, new shopping centres, new hospitals, new university buildings, new playing fields and parks have been added, yet nothing has been done well. 'Nothing has been done well in Oxford for nearly a hundred years. And this in a city where for hundreds of years previously most things had been done especially well.'

He blames the University as well as the Corporation and the County Councils as well as the City. 'No longer able to create the good we let the bad just happen. The city today shows all the marks of timidity, hesitation, lack of high purpose and resolve. It reflects the indecision, the littleness of spirit of all concerned in its development.'

In 1801 the population of Oxford was 12,000. When I was an undergraduate in 1905–1909 it had reached 60,000. Today it is well over 100,000. It sounds difficult to believe but as things are Oxford provides a satisfactory home for less than two-thirds of its population.

It is not only undergraduates who have to double up and share their rooms, young married couples have to share houses and flats, often with their in-laws. The result is that a very high percentage of Oxford workers are to all intents and purposes homeless. They count themselves lucky to be able to have a roof over their heads at night, but they have no homes.

The main cause of the congestion is, of course, the presence of the Nuffield organization and the Pressed Steel Company which employ some 17,000 workers.

'There are', says Mr Sharp 'no geographical, social, or economic reasons why these two great industries should be in Oxford. On the contrary there are a great many reasons why they should not. They came to Oxford only because Lord Nuffield lived there. The great Nuffield works are an extension of a shed in a back garden. The Pressed Steel Works are an extension again of these. None of the raw materials used by either undertaking is drawn from the Oxford locality, except a little woodwork. Much of their labour came in from other parts of the country for no other reason than to find work of any sort in a period of national depression. Few of the finished products remain in Oxford. The development of these works in Oxford was the purest accident. It is rarely that so enormous an industry has developed in so unsuitable a locality.'

The numbers working in the University and employed by the colleges far outweigh the number of industrial workers, but the City as a whole is inadequately served in the matter of cultural entertainment. The New Theatre is, after the Shakespeare Memorial Theatre at Stratford, the best appointed theatre in the provinces, and during term provides excellent entertainment. In the vacation it degenerates into a Music Hall. There are three large cinemas in the city centre, all owned by one circuit. There is no adequate Art Gallery, no Concert Hall, no Assembly Rooms, no public lecture hall. There are, it is true about 2,000 shops, but nearly half of these lie to the East of Magdalen Bridge and are therefore not in the city at all.

The quality of some of these shops, notably the bookshops and some of the tailors, is unusually high as we should expect in a University, but compared with other towns of the same size there are too few shops and these are not outstanding.

C

It is understandable that the majority of shops cater primarily for the needs of undergraduates, but the day is gone for ever when undergraduates could afford to run up bills and be extravagant in their tastes. The majority of those in residence today are paid by the Government to be up, and in any event under our existing laws very few people are allowed to earn enough money to pay for the education of their children.

But even if the undergraduates and general public are impoverished the tourists from overseas are not, and it is astonishing to find that this Mecca of all tourists from all over the world not only provides scarcely any accommodation but has nothing to sell except a view of the colleges.

Everyone who has travelled agrees that when you have discovered them there are parts of Oxford, the Parks, St John's Gardens, Christ Church Meadows, Magdalen Tower, Mesopotamia, the Upper River, Tom Quad, that are unmatchable anywhere in the world, but as soon as the visitor has done this brief round of sight-seeing he will be well advised to make for Bath or some other city where the authorities have gone to the trouble to look after the comfort of the tourist and provide him with good hotels and inviting shops.

Far too much of Oxford is squalid. The majority of visitors come to Oxford by train. The two stations in Oxford have to be seen to be believed. One of these is a terminus, connecting only with Bletchley and bears all the marks of a hastily run-up shack in a gold-mining outpost in Alaska that has been long deserted.

Many passengers appear to come and go, but if there is a staff it is practically never visible.

The adjoining Western Region station consists of two long platforms and it is a very important centre indeed as it lies on a route that connects the North and West, that is Birkenhead, Chester and Birmingham, as well as York, Sheffield, Rugby, Leicester, and Cheltenham, both with London and the South and South-West.

The service to London is good. The distance is about 60 miles and the time taken is about 75 minutes. There are also occasional good cross-country connections. Where the Western Region station fails is not in service – the employees are invariably courteous (in peace time) – but in the ugliness and inadequacy of its buildings. It sometimes takes almost as long to leave the station as it does to come from Reading.

There are no signs whatever that we have reached the fairest city in the world. The road leading from the station to the High Street is remarkable only for the prison and a number of haphazardly placed warehouses and derelict places.

The gasworks certainly take the eye, but one looks in vain for the serried series of noble spires of which there is so much talk. Cooper's marmalade factory hides what is to my mind the barest and ugliest cattle market in England which is bounded by a ditch full of discarded tins and motor tyres overlooked by a slum in which Thomas Hardy with his unfailing eye for the fitting placed the unhappy Jude the Obscure.

When at length you reach the double bottle-neck of Carfax, you will have no time (if you are on foot or bicycle) to look out for any sign of an ancient city or university, you will be too busy watching the traffic lights and being swept across the street in the tide of the rest of the swirling crowd.

To the north lies Cornmarket Street, known to everyone as 'The Corn', the pavements of which are so thronged with shoppers that there is an inevitable spill over into the road which is already overcrowded with buses, lorries, bicycles and cars. This is the main shopping street and possesses one dignified Georgian building, the Clarendon, once an hotel, then a propping-up place for American soldiers and now bought by Woolworth's who already own a store on the opposite side of the road. Hidden in one alley stands the ugly pseudo-Gothic University Union, the famous Debating Society to which nearly all undergraduates belong, and hidden in another is a medieval courtyard with balconies, the too little-known Golden Cross hotel, the least assuming and most satisfying of all Oxford's hostelries and the favourite haunt in late years of Hilaire Belloc and James Agate.

To the south of Carfax lies St Aldate's (pronounced St Old's), which contains the Victorian Town Hall, City Library, Post Office, Police Station and outstandingly noble Tudor front of Christ Church, always known as the House ('Aedes Christi'), the great gateway of which is surmounted by a Tower added by Sir Christopher Wren.

In the belfry of this tower stands Great Tom, a deeply resonant bell that rings 101 times nightly at five minutes past nine to remind the world that Christ Church once contained 101 students. The word student now stands for Senior Members, Doctors of the House, not undergraduates.

Christ Church jealously preserves its own traditions. It is not in the ordinary sense a college, and no one who wishes to be thought *au fait* with University etiquette ever falls into the error of speaking of Christ Church College. There is no such place. The Dean of Christ Church is Dean of the Diocese of Oxford as well as Head of the House, and undergraduates use the Cathedral, which stands on the further side of Tom Quad, as their Chapel.

The bells of this Cathedral spire do not strike at the hour or the half hour, they strike at five minutes and thirty-five minutes past the hour.

All other colleges finally lock their gates at midnight. Christ Church alone remains open till 12.20 a.m., a privilege which causes considerable heart-burnings among members of less fortunate colleges, especially at dances.

Folly Bridge which spans the Thames lies at the south side of St Aldate's and beyond the bridge sprawl the unimaginative rows of small houses and Council estates of Hinksey.

To the east of Carfax stands one of the most famous streets in the world, High Street, commonly known as the High.

It is exquisitely curved in the shape of a boomerang and contains not only the Italianate front of St Mary's, the University church, but also the fronts of Brasenose, All Souls, Queen's, Magdalen, Oriel, University College, the dignified Examination Schools, and the Botanical Gardens.

For architectural beauty it has no rival in the British Isles, probably not in the world. I am lucky enough to remember a time forty years ago when it was possible to stand and appreciate the beauty of the twin peaks of All Souls and the majesty of Magdalen Tower in peace and quietude. There was no noise more raucous than that of the horse-drawn trams, which could always be boarded while in motion.

Today I take my life in my hands whenever I have to pay a call at my Bank or elect to have luncheon at Vincent's Club which lie on the further side from my house. The traffic never lets up from dawn to dusk, and only when the moon is up on our way home from a 'Commem' Ball at four or five in the morning is it still possible to recapture the ancient rapture that we used to feel in that once lovely street.

Broad Street, commonly known as the Broad, which runs almost parallel to the north, is in better case. It is, as its name implies broad and there is usually room enough and time enough to wonder at the anomalies of archi-tecture which here confront the eye. These include the new Bodleian, a massive brick cube of austerity which adequately interprets the age of utilitarian mechanism, and the Lewis Museum, a Tudor gem which is apt to be over-looked by reason of the fact that it hides behind a row of unrecognizable stone heads that are reputed to be of Roman emperors, but have been eaten away by wind and rain almost as satisfactorily as if they had been gibbeted human heads.

Trinity's fine iron gates do much to restore the balance on the other side of the road, but it would be difficult to think of an uglier frontage than that of Trinity's neighbour, Balliol, until you travel down the Parks Road to Keble about whose variegated brick work it is difficult to find a printable epithet.

A narrow medieval one-way street links the High and the Broad. This is Turl Street, known as the Turl, and in it stand on the one side Jesus, and on the other Lincoln and Exeter.

The colleges bear no resemblance to colleges in the United States. Instead of each college standing in its own spacious campus, the Oxford colleges, so far as the men's colleges are concerned are all huddled together more or less inside the city walls, and cover little more than a quarter of a square mile. All the playing fields are a great way off, many of them on the other side of the river. The women's colleges are in better case as they all lie far outside the city walls, all but one in North Oxford.

In a world where everything has changed with such bewildering rapidity during the last thirty years it could scarcely be hoped that Oxford would remain the same, but we are still apt to think of it as the home of lost causes, holding itself a little aloof from the general world confusion.

The truth is that instead of changing less than other places, it has undergone a great upheaval. There used to be a rivalry between Town and Gown, which led to bloodshed in medieval times, but resolved itself into such relatively harmless encounters as the letting loose of rats in the High and the seizure of policemen's helmets when I was an undergraduate. Today the fight, as Mr Sharp points out, is between gown and dungarees.

Oxford has allowed itself to become just another industrial city like Walsall, Wednesbury and Coventry. There may be no harm in industrial cities as such, but there is a great deal of harm when Oxford, the world's outstanding stronghold of culture, joins the herd. It is good for business to harbour industries. It is extremely bad for the precious spirit that is Oxford.

The University is in danger of being submerged. It is already unwieldy. It is already set for becoming a minor English Detroit, which fills anyone who knows Detroit with grave misgivings.

The only possible advantage which could accrue to Oxford if it allowed itself to grow as large as Middlesbrough is that it would be rich enough to buy a professional team of footballers as good as those who represent Middlesbrough but there are still living a quite large number of people who do not depend for their living on the results of football pools.

What Oxford needs is a decline, not an increase of population, an elimination of the nerve-racking turmoil, and the time-wasting congestion. On an ordinary mid-week day 35,000 vehicles endeavour to cross Carfax in the twelve hours between eight in the morning and eight at night. Nearly half the population, nearly 50,000 of them, not only own bicycles but ride them to and from work or shopping. Cyclists in Oxford are not a swarm, they are a plague.

There are by-passes, but one of them remains unfinished, and the other is still a quiet country road. Every driver of brick-laden lorries, aeroplane scraps, furniture vans, market produce or livestock insists on driving through the heart of Oxford, impelled perhaps by a desire to see its architectural beauty.

It is this fact that makes me fear that even if Mr Sharp's recommendation of the opening of Merton Mall through the Broad Walk of Christ Church Meadows were adopted, the new road would not be universally adopted and the meadows would lose their quietude without materially helping the High to regain her ancient peace.

Why Cathedral cities should possess worse slums than other towns I do not know, unless it is that most cities are medieval in origin. The fact remains that in St Ebbe's, opposite Christ Church, there are nearly 4,000 houses that are a disgrace to any civilized nation. The whole of St Ebbe's needs to be pulled down.

Adequate rehousing is one of Oxford's most pressing needs, whether for townsmen or gownsmen.

Every one of the 28 colleges is overcrowded, and the system of licensed lodgings for senior undergraduates has collapsed. Undergraduates may now live where they like. The result is that a great part of the term and indeed part of the vacation is spent by undergraduates searching for a roof to cover them after their one year or two years in college is finished.

So desperate is the need that there has been talk of moving large parts of the University out to Wytham, a hillside some three miles to the north-west, but this would produce a University as suburban as that of Birmingham and undoubtedly prove fatal to that special kind of education that Oxford boasts of providing 'an education in living as well as in learning'. Oxford stands or falls as a University where she now is. So for that matter does the city, and if you do not know Oxford well you may well be surprised to learn that among her immediate requirements are a new Town Hall, Public Assembly Halls, Library, Art Gallery, City Museum, Welfare Centre, Municipal College, County Council offices and Law Courts, the existing public buildings being hopelessly inadequate as well as being inartistic.

Mr Sharp's plan is to build all these new Civic Buildings to the west of Carfax. The present shopping centre is to remain where it is except for the covered market which houses all the central retail shops for meat and most of those for fruit and vegetables. It is proposed to move this also to the west side of Carfax.

One of the most curious features of Oxford is the fact that no attempt has ever been made to take advantage of the fact that it lies on the Thames. Every other Thames-side resort has hotels with lawns facing the river. Oxford has none.

All the notice that Oxford takes of the Thames where the College crews race twice every year, in Torpids and Eights Weeks, is to line the north bank with College barges.

The south bank is an ideal site for a series of much needed riverside hotels. There are no riverside restaurants, and no clean bathing-pools.

The Cherwell contains two reserved reaches known as Parson's Pleasure and Dame's Delight which could only afford pleasure or delight to those who like bathing in duck weed. An inlet of the Thames known as Long Bridges is always overcrowded when the water is warm enough to bathe in, and the only chance of relatively clean water and quietude is in the waters of the Upper River above Godstow about three miles from the centre of the city.

As Oxford is extremely well irrigated, and for weeks during the winter uncomfortably submerged it seems strange indeed that no provision has been made to provide an up to date open air swimming pool with specially cleansed water.

Many English and Welsh towns still retain traces of their medieval walls, notably York, Chester, Tenby, Conway and Sandwich. Considerable stretches of her walls survive in Oxford, but the only stretch that is quite clear of buildings is the southern section that runs above Deadman's Walk and acts as a boundary between Merton and Christ Church Meadows.

The first sector is that which bounds the gardens of New College where the ramparts, bastions and walls all rise to their full height and are in a remarkably fine state of preservation.

Unfortunately only the inner, college side lies open. The public side is obscured by a number of houses built right up to the walls themselves, and these certainly should be laid bare.

It ought not be difficult to open a horizontal barrier of open spaces where the vertical barrier has disappeared, and once more reveal to the public exactly what were the limits of the ancient city.

Mr Sharp's plan is simple. It is to preserve the old city east of Carfax with its colleges revealed and to build a new city west of Carfax not unworthy of the old.

At the extreme west end will be the Central Transport Depot, a railway station run in conjunction with a vast bus station.

At present long-distance buses all start from Gloucester Green and in view of the fact that this is a bus junction for routes to Liverpool, Bedford, South Wales, Portsmouth, Southampton, London, Winchester, Cardiff, Cheltenham,

Birmingham and Bristol it is odd that it should compare so unfavourably with the bus station at Cheltenham.

At present there are not only no shelters for waiting passengers, but no indicators to tell passengers where they ought to stand, with the result that very few people in Oxford realize that there are buses running to nearly every considerable English and Welsh town.

In the matter of stone the colleges have been lucky in their colour, unlucky in their durability. The local Headington stone of which so many colleges were built wears away with such rapidity that some colleges, notably Christ Church and Magdalen are constantly being refaced, a very costly process.

Merton added on a series of expensive buildings in 1938 of stone from Clipsham that is not only warm and light in appearance but is as durable as granite. Other colleges have now followed suit, and there is little chance of the Magdalen or St John's gargoyles degenerating into the moth-eaten aspect of the Roman Emperors that face the Broad.

If Mr Sharp's plans are adopted the Oxford of tomorrow will be a manageable city of some 90,000 inhabitants, relieved of the burden of the Nuffield organization and the Pressed Steel Works, functioning mainly as a University and county capital, with well balanced and well diversified industries, with new by-passes, a middle ring road, new inner city roads, new railway stations, bus station and Civic Offices, all on the West side of Carfax, doubled hotel accommodation mainly on the Thames banks, new riverside open spaces, and new tree planting in the suburbs.

'It is', he says 'a plan to preserve old beauty and to make new beauty possible: to add new convenience: to achieve, for the first time in the history of the city, a social balance and a functional equilibrium.'

Everyone who loves Oxford and has the interest of the city at heart will give *Oxford Replanned* a very careful hearing.

What steps can be taken to force the hand of the City Councillors to take action I do not know.

This is not an age, unfortunately, when the claims of aesthetic beauty are allowed a place on any Council's agenda, but if the opportunity to replan Oxford is not immediately seized the Oxford we knew and loved will soon cease to be. Her decline will be as swift and final as that of our country houses.

The Radcliffe Camera and St Mary's Church

The Cloister, All Souls College

College Barges on the Thames

CHAPTER II

Some Opinions of Oxford

It is the most noble theatre and Emporium of all Sciences. The most noble Athens, the Muses' seat, and one of England's stays, nay the sun, the eye and the soul thereof. The very source and most clear spring of good literature and wisdom, from whence religion, civility and learning are spread most plenteously into all parts of the Realm.

ANTHONY À WOOD

To the University of Oxford I acknowledge no obligation: and she will as cheerfully renounce me for a son as I am willing to disclaim her from a mother. I spent fourteen months at Magdalen College: they proved the fourteen months the most idle, unprofitable of my whole life : . . . The schools of Oxford and Cambridge were founded in a dark age of false and barbarous science: and they are still tainted with the vices of their origin . . . As a gentleman commoner I was admitted to the Society of the fellows – their conversation stagnated in a round of College business and Tory politics, personal anecdotes, and private scandal: their dull and deep potations excused the brisk intemperance of youth: the sum of my improvement in the University of Oxford is confined to three or four Latin plays.

EDMUND GIBBON

Long continuance in those places (Oxford and Cambridge) is either a sign of lack of friends or of learning.

HARRISON

The Universities, Oxford especially, have been unhappily successful in corrupting the principles of those who were sent to be bred in them.

BISHOP BURNET

If Oxford is not highbrow, what on earth is Oxford?

BERNARD SHAW

We would pass our lives in Oxford without having or wanting any other idea – that of the place is enough.

WILLIAM HAZLITT

Upon beholding the masses of buildings, at Oxford, devoted to what they call 'learning', I could not help reflecting on the drones that they contain and the wasps they send forth. The great and prevalent characteristic is folly: emptiness of head: want of talent: and one half of the fellows who are what are called educated here are unfit to be clerks in a grocer's or mercer's shop.

WILLIAM COBBETT

Whispering from the towers the last enchantments of the Middle Ages . . . Home of lost causes, and forsaken beliefs, and unpopular names and impossible loyalties.

MATTHEW ARNOLD

This university is the greatest of human institutions.

LORD SIMON

The home of dead languages and undying prejudices.

JOHN BRIGHT

A painted lady, from whom Labour has nothing to expect.

RAMSEY MACDONALD

There is a charm about Oxford which tells on one, a certain freshness and independence and besides a certain geniality of life such as one does not find elsewhere.

J. R. GREEN

I nauseate Christ Church and will never live more among such people who now have the prevailing power there.

HUMPHREY PRIDEAUX

Oxford still remains the most beautiful thing in England.

OSCAR WILDE

The most beautiful place in the world where young men go to live in colleges for six months in the year in order to have a good time, learn a little and take a degree which is regarded as a certificate of gentility and entitles them to votes for two Members of Parliament and to veto all improvements in the method and organization of the University.

RAY LANKESTER

Dear Oxford.

QUEEN ELIZABETH

Oxford, a very sweet place, mighty fine and well seated, and cheap entertainment.

SAMUEL PEPYS

The Oxford man looks as if the world belongs to him: the Cambridge man as if he did not care to whom it belonged.

ANON.

Oxford, ancient mother, I owe thee nothing. For the first two years of my residence, I did not utter one hundred words.

THOMAS DE QUINCEY

Of all the months of my life (happily they did not amount to years) those which were passed at Oxford were the most unprofitable. What Greek I took there, I literally left there. All I learnt was a little swimming and a little boating.

ROBERT SOUTHEY

My Oxford career culminated in a total and scandalous failure.

A. L. SWINBURNE

He had no rooms in college, went little to it, was no sportsman, belonged to no set, went to a few lectures and was warned about his idleness.

About CECIL RHODES

Oxford is no good air.

ANTHONY À WOOD

CHAPTER III

The History of Oxford

The Medieval University

CHRIST CHURCH is not the oldest college but it stands on the site of an ancient Saxon convent and the collegiate church of St George within the Castle as well as the abbeys of Eynsham and Osney brought clerks to Oxford in early Norman days. Indeed we know that Henry I, who built a palace at Beaumont, delighted in their conversation. Theobald of Etampes, a master from Caen, was teaching in Oxford before 1117 and Robert Pullen and Vacarius, the great Lombard jurist were teaching here before 1150. In the second half of the twelfth century there appears to have been a sudden development into homes for masters and scholars gathering from all over Europe, especially in Bologna and Paris, in which the Universities, or whole body, established coporate organizations with peculiar customs and privileges of their own. Paris under Abelard became the first city of teaching and Englishmen went over in large numbers.

In 1167 foreign students were driven out of Paris and Henry II also in his quarrel with St Thomas à Becket stopped the flow of English clerks across the Channel.

As the schools in Oxford grew rapidly after 1170 it is reasonable to infer that the principal cause was the transference of students from Paris.

History is in some measure repeating itself in this respect, for an anonymous French benefactor has recently given £1,500,000 towards the endowment of a new college which will undoubtedly contain many students from France. Most of the early Oxford customs emanated from Paris.

A degree originally was nothing more or less than a licence to teach and the chief object of study as well as the chief aim of the scholastic debates was to reconcile the teaching of the Church with the growing demands of philosophy and learning. Latin was the language of the Church. Logic was used to explain theology. Plato was read in order to elucidate the nature of God. Aristotle helped to elucidate the problems of faith. But the Oxford masters had a remarkable degree of independence. The Chancellor was the Bishop's representative, but the Bishop was at Lincoln, which gave him the chance of asserting his independence.

A sharp quarrel between Church and State arose in 1208–9 as the result of two clerks being hanged by the townsmen, who in spite of being backed by King John had to yield.

In 1214 came the famous ordinance of the Pope which gave the University of Oxford its first charter. By this ordinance the townsmen were compelled to limit their rents and to pay tribute to the University for ever. That payment, taken over by the Treasury, still continues, and the University Chest still receives it.

In spite of or because of this there was a good deal of disorder.

In 1238 a mob attacked a papal legate, and in 1244 and 1268 there were quarrels with the Jews who were both rich and powerful.

In 1252, 1274 and 1334 there were riots between the Northerners and Southerners and Town and Gown battles ended with the lanes round St Mary's running with blood.

Indeed one of these riots, in 1264, led to a secession of students, which was followed in 1334 by a much greater secession to Stamford when the students carried off the brazen nose of Brasenose with them.

In 1298 the townsmen complained to the King that the criminals of two counties made Oxford their headquarters and wore the robes of Oxford clerks.

In 1355, on St Scholastica's Day, the country people broke into the halls and burnt them down, even attacking a procession of friars and throwing down their crucifix. But on each of these occasions, the University, backed by the King and the Church, emerged stronger than before. The Royal Charters strengthened their position and after the slaughter of 1355 the Chancellor acquired supreme power over both the trade and independence of the town.

Hundreds of students, drawn from all ranks of life, in the main poor and very young, began to collect in Schools Street by St Mary's Church.

There were in the thirteenth century, probably about 1,300 students, the number falling to 600 after the Black Death. They lived in lodgings, inns and halls. Fees were low and living cheap. Eightpence a week covered the cost of commons: most clerks had two meals a day with a plentiful supply of beer and meat. Fires on the other hand were rare, but the student could count on a bed, table, chest, sufficient clothes, a lute or harp, a knife, sword or bow and arrows. There were both militant and sporting, for we hear a good deal of their cockfighting and poaching, and most of them kept dogs, hawks and ferrets in spite of discouragement by the authorities.

Ball games and dancing were vigorously denounced, but it was less easy to put a stop to drinking and singing. The singing seems to have been evenly divided between the devotional and the bawdy.

In those early days the centre of University life was St Mary's Church. It was not till 1320 that the Old House of Congregation, built by a Bishop of Worcester to the north east of the church, gave the university an habitation of its own. The Library occupied the first floor and the Lesser Congregation of teachers met on the ground floor. The fine Divinity School was added in 1430 by an Abbot of Osney. The Great Congregation continued to meet in the Choir of St Mary's, and the Black Congregation, the Faculty of Arts met in St Mildred's

It was in St Mary's that the first recorded Master of Arts, afterwards Archbishop and Saint received his degree, and in St Mary's that the early Chancellors, including Thomas de Cantelupe, used to preside. We first hear of Proctors in 1248.

The subjects taught were the Seven Liberal arts, the Trivium, Grammar, Rhetoric and Dialectic, included Latin and Logic, a certain amount of philology and the Elements of Roman Law, and the Quadrivium Music, Arithmetic, Geometry and Astronomy. They read Cicero, Ovid, Virgil, Terence, Livy, Tacitus and Lucan. Arithmetic together with Astronomy helped to fix ecclesiastical dates. Geometry was based on Euclid, Astronomy on the Ptolemaic system in which the sun and the planets revolved round the earth. It was of course closely linked with astrology because many men believed that the stars affected man's destiny as readers of the less literate press apparently still believe today.

The Seven Arts were supplemented by the three Philosophies, Natural Philosophy which explained the world of science, Moral Philosophy which probed into the mysteries of duty, conscience and will, and Metaphysical Philosophy which dealt with the origin and future of mankind. In every department of study Aristotle was accepted as the final authority.

For two years students attended lectures and learned to debate. The disputations of his third year led to Responsions in his fourth. He then proceeded to Determination, satisfied the examiners that he had read the books and proved himself able to dispute. He then became Bachelor, and after three more years received his Master's degree and was then considered qualified to teach.

If he wished to study Medicine, Law or Theology he had to spend more years at the University. Theology was reckoned as the premier science.

In 1221 the Dominicans came over as preachers in the Jewry to be followed within three years by the Franciscans. In 1244 the Grey Friars were given permission by the King to break through the south wall of Oxford and build themselves a home among the marshes of the Thames.

Robert Grosseteste was among those who taught in the Friars' Schools and Roger Bacon, a disciple of Grosseteste, became so powerful that he was accounted a magician.

The Carmelites followed the Franciscans in Beaumont, and the Augustinians in Smith Gate.

Thomas Aquinas set out to prove that Aristotle and Plato were forerunners of the Christian faith and about 1300 John Duns Scotus came over to lecture for the Franciscans.

John Wycliffe, Master of Balliol in 1360, was not a friar but a reformer who sought to cure the abuses that had crept into the medieval church. He had a great following and his prose translation of the Bible was received with enthusiasm by his Oxford pupils. It was a long time before Archbishop Arundel and his successors were able to stamp out Wycliffe's movement for a reform of the Church.

In the fifteenth century the Great Schism in the Papacy caused a rapid decline in the influence of the Church. The halls of Oxford decayed and their numbers went down. There was again disorder followed by the Wars of the Roses, in which Oxford supported the Lancastrian cause.

In spite however of poverty Oxford continued to expand her buildings. There was the new Divinity School with the new library endowed with Duke Humphrey's fine collection of books, St Mary's was rebuilt, new Chests were founded, and a Press set up in the High Street for printing Oxford books. By the time that Richard III visited the University in 1483 he found a new spirit.

The end of the Middle Ages was at hand.

The Early Colleges

In 1280 money bequeathed in 1249 by William of Durham to support masters of arts studying theology was devoted to the foundation of University College, a society of fair masters.

Some time after 1255, John Balliol established a small community of scholars, which is mentioned in June 1266, and in 1262 Walter de Merton, bishop and statesman, attempted the building of a college better endowed and organized than any other. Merton was in consequence easily the most important of the early colleges though Balliol's scholars were in residence first.

These early colleges were not built on any definite plan. The scholars had to have somewhere to sleep and live, a hall to eat and drink in, a kitchen to cook in, a chapel, a chest for manuscripts and a safe place for documents.

Queen's built a gate-house, New College a tower and was the first college to have a regular quadrangle, with a brewhouse, bakehouse, cloisters, bell-tower and adjoining garden. But William of Wykeham had more money at his disposal than the others. Merton, as the result of a fair endowment, built an unusually noble chapel. Indeed its thirteenth century choir is one of the out-standing architectural features of the University. The transepts are of later date and the nave was never even begun. The huge bell-tower was furnished in 1451.

The hall is contemporary with the chapel choir, and is Merton's crowning glory. Mob Quad, with its steep-pitched roof and chain library, is as old as anything in the college. This library was given to the college in the fourteenth century by Bishop Rede. The origin of the word 'Mob' is unknown.

Neither Balliol nor University College can show any comparable buildings, for it was not until the fifteenth century that Balliol began to take shape, and it was not till the seventeenth and eighteenth centuries that the quadrangles fronting the High replaced the earlier buildings of University College.

There were two other thirteenth century colleges which owed their foundations to the monks. The cell for Benedictine monks from Gloucester, established by John Giffard in 1283 developed into a college for students of that order, and their monastic buildings can still be seen woven into the texture of what is now Worcester College. Three years later the Durham monks established a house for their students, the remains of which have been incorporated into the Trinity of today.

Several new colleges came into being in the fourteenth century, four of which have survived.

Walter de Stapeldon founded Exeter in 1314 for poor arts students from the west country. It acquired new statutes and a second founder in the reign of Queen Elizabeth.

About 1414 Adam de Brome, Rector of St Mary's, founded Oriel to train scholars in theology and the art of dialectic. Two years later Edward II re-founded it and then Bishop Burghersh provided it with yet another lot of statutes. It acquired shops and houses close by St Mary's and the old lepers' hospital of St Bartholomew outside the town. Its most important tenement, La Oriole, secured in 1329, gave it its name.

The Queen's College, founded in 1341 by Robert of Eglesfield, was kept going and given further endowments by Queen Philippa who secured the

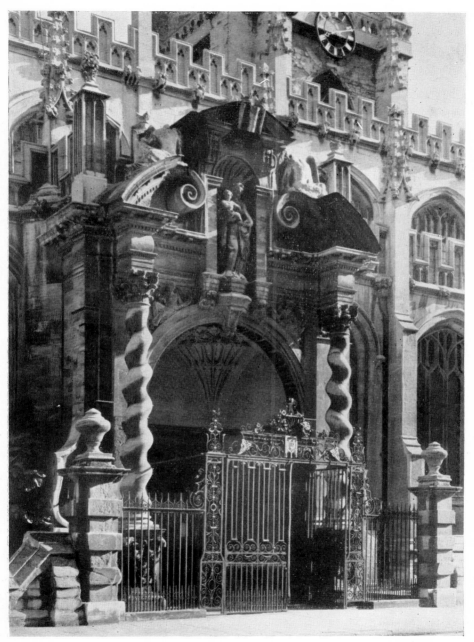

The South Porch, St Mary's Church

Tom Quad and the Cathedral, Christ Church

The Fellows' Quadrangle, Merton College

property of God's House in Southampton to enable it to continue. The medieval buildings behind the houses in the High Street were later demolished.

William of Wykeham procured a charter in 1379. In 1387 his seventy poor scholars were installed in their stately home which had not only ample space but could rely on his already famous school at Winchester for endowments and pupils.

New College was destined to set the fashion for nearly all the later colleges. The scholars were intended to study chiefly theology and law, to serve both Church and State.

New College emphatically stood for the old order strengthened by education. It still does.

The students of Merton set the example for the introduction of the collegiate system and the statutes of New College fell into line with the Merton plan.

The four masters of arts at University College received fifty shillings a year for maintenance and were intended to study theology. The first members of Balliol and Exeter were undergraduate students in arts, and at Merton the majority were expected after their arts course to study theology, but 'some men of humility' might be allowed to substitute Canon Law.

Each college soon began to develop its own peculiar characteristics.

Merton trained not only ecclesiastics and lawyers, but mathematicians, astronomers and medical men.

University had a master who served under Henry V at Agincourt, Palmer, the builder of the fine tower at Exeter was court physician to Margaret of Anjou. The Early Lancastrian Princes were at Queen's, Archbishop Arundel was a commoner of Oriel, while Archbishops Chichele and Cranley were Fellows of New College.

Other colleges were founded in the fifteenth century. Lincoln came into being in 1429 owing to the good offices of Bishop Fleming, but it was refounded 50 years later by Rotherham, Bishop of Lincoln.

All Souls was founded in 1438 by Archbishop Chichele as a memorial to the men who fell at Agincourt. It possessed forty fellows, sixteen of whom were law students. Its endowment came mainly from suppressed priories.

William of Waynflete founded Magdalen in 1458 on the site of the old Hospital of St John outside the town. He was Master of Eton, and later Bishop and Lord Chancellor. He established not only the college but also the Grammar School by its side and provided not only for forty fellows, but for thirty more younger foundationers, called *demi-socii* or demies. He also encouraged the admission of Commoners not on the foundation.

E

Twenty 'sons of nobles and of worthy persons' were to be allowed to go up to Magdalen at their own expense.

Here is a proof of the longevity of college tradition, for Magdalen has always been a resort of the sons of nobles, sharing that distinction with Christ Church.

THE TUDOR AGE

As might be expected the Renaissance and Reformation changed the whole outlook of Oxford.

Before the end of the fifteenth century Grocyn and Linacre, Latimer and Lily had come back from Italy fired with enthusiasm for the New Learning. John Colet of Magdalen was already applying the doctrines of Savonarola to education and religion. Erasmus found congenial companionship in the society both of Colet and Sir Thomas More.

Wolsey, an undergraduate of Magdalen, never forgot Oxford, but came back to build the most magnificent of all colleges which the King confiscated and finished after the Cardinal fell from grace. Cardinal College, licensed in 1525 was intended by Wolsey to house 177 students with a revenue of £2,000 a year. He laid out Tom Quad, the largest and noblest of all college quadrangles, built a stupendous kitchen, one of the Seven Wonders of Oxford, and a Hall that compares favourably with the Great Hall of Westminster. His plan for a chapel, commensurate with his other schemes, had to be abandoned and the House had to be content with the ancient church of St Frideswide's. It was, however, not till 1546 that Christ Church took its permanent form.

An Oxford bishopric had then been formed by Henry VIII endowed with the spoils of Osney Abbey. The Dean and Canons took over Wolsey's buildings. They staffed the Cathedral and provided professors for the University. They ruled a vast establishment of 101 students, with chaplains, singing men, bedesmen, retainers and commoners. By a curious oversight Christ Church failed to receive any statutes, so she remains a law unto herself, the relations between the Chapter and the College remaining undefined and unique. The spirit of the New Learning spread from Colet, More, Erasmus and Wolsey in all directions.

Bishop Fox, for instance, founded Corpus Christi College in 1517 largely to encourage the new classical training. It still preserves a tradition for classicism. He gave his twenty scholars ample endowments, appointed a President, John Claymond, who was the leading Latin scholar of his day, built a lovely

THE HISTORY OF OXFORD

quadrangle, and a fine library which is typical of the college library of the Renaissance. His statutes provided for a teaching in Greek and Latin so liberal that Erasmus prophesied that Corpus would soon become one of the chief glories of Britain.

Two other college founders of that era had other ideas, Bishop Smyth and Sir Richard Sutton took possession of Brasenose Hall, one of the oldest and most renowned of the halls, and founded in 1512 a new college for the study of philosophy, logic and sophistry as a training for theology. And the resulting college of Brasenose has had a career at least as honourable as that of Corpus, though its members are more given to a convivial life and strenuous physical exercise.

Oxford acquiesced a little uneasily in the breach with Rome.

Cromwell appointed two Commissioners to visit the University who showed scant respect either for the schoolmen or the monks, but they did make provision for new teaching in Greek and Latin, Medicine and Civil Law.

Monastic property had, of course, been seized by the King.

St Frideswide's and Littlemore had gone to endow Cardinal College. Abingdon, Osney, Newby, Eynsham, and Godstow were all despoiled.

The colleges that depended for their endowments on Gloucester, Durham, and Canterbury fell with the houses that had maintained them. All the monastic colleges and settlements of friars were confiscated, Franciscans, Dominicans, Carmelites and Augustinians all sharing the common fate.

The University had no alternative but to submit to the dictates of Cromwell, Cranmer and Somerset.

The Protestant Reformers swept away all emblems of superstition, statues, stained glass windows, manuscripts and missals.

It was with a better grace that when the tide turned the University submitted to Bishop Gardiner and Cardinal Pole. Ridley, Latimer and Cranmer went to the stake, but Elizabeth's first Parliament soon repealed the laws of Bloody Mary.

New colleges were established in the buildings of the old monks.

Durham College passed into the hands of Sir Thomas Pope, a wealthy Tudor politician. Gloucester College and St Bernard's went to Sir Thomas White, a rich merchant. Wadham was established in the quarters of the Austin Friars. Pope founded Trinity in 1555 with a president, twelve fellows and eight scholars. White, a patron of the Merchant Taylors' School, founded St Johns' College in the grounds and buildings of St Bernard's College in the same year.

As may be imagined there were sharp controversies between the colleges.

Dean Sampson of Christ Church and President Humfrey of Magdalen were staunch Puritans. Town and Gown quarrelled as violently as ever. There was a violent plague in 1571 and a worse one in 1577. But it is worth noting that when the young Queen Elizabeth visited Oxford in 1566 and spent six days receiving homage and seeing plays she was everywhere welcomed with a passionate loyalty that was as sincere as it was universal.

Leicester as Chancellor sought to remedy the want of discipline, the neglect of lectures, the drinking, dicing, card-playing and growing extravagance in dress by enforcing a new set of rules.

The Matriculation Statute of 1565 established a Register, as the result of which all scholars had to be enrolled under a master or tutor in some hall or college. In 1581 a new statute made it compulsory for all students to subscribe to the thirty-nine articles and the Queen's Supremacy.

Of the old halls only eight, Broadgates and Hart Hall, St Albans, St Mary's and St Edmund's, Magdalen Hall, Gloucester Hall and New Inn Hall survived.

There were in 1570 some 1,700 members of the University and in 1571 both Oxford and Cambridge were incorporated by Act of Parliament.

Undergraduates were still very young (Wolsey took his Mastership at fourteen) and for the first time included the well-to-do. From being a poor man's university Oxford became fashionable, like Eton and Winchester, Sherborne and other Public Schools which had been founded to provide education for the local poor. Undergraduates became luxurious in habits and vain in dress.

There was a remarkable enthusiasm for drama, not unlike that in our own time when it is proposed to build a £300,000 Oxford University Theatre for the encouragement of Drama. The report on this, recently published by the Oxford Press at 7s 6d, gives the findings of the Commission financed by Sir Alexander Korda and if the project is carried out will mean that Oxford will have the most progressive and handsomest theatre in the country.

Queen Elizabeth, James I and Charles I all saw plays acted in Christ Church Hall. In all fairness, however, it must be conceded that the University wits of the Elizabethan stage nearly all came from Cambridge; Christopher Marlowe, Robert Greene, Thomas Lodge, and Edmund Spenser were all Cambridge men. Oxford had to rest content with 'Euphues' Lyly. No one has been able to explain why through the centuries Cambridge has always been the nest of singing birds, producing among other poets Milton, Byron, Wordsworth, Tennyson, Herrick, Marvell, Drayton, Spenser, Coleridge, Marlowe, while Oxford had to be content with Shelley, Matthew Arnold, Beddoes, Bridges, Robert Hugh Clough, Southey and John Betjeman.

When Elizabeth returned to Oxford in 1592 she found Protestantism firmly established. The Puritan influence was particularly strong, not only at Christ Church and Magdalen, but also at Balliol, Exeter, Queen's and Corpus. Yet there had been Oxford men, Father Campion was one, who had been martyred for his Catholic faith, and William Allen of Oriel had founded Douai.

During her reign Sir Walter Raleigh passed through Oriel and Sir Philip Sidney added lustre to Christ Church. Archbishop Laud was then an undergraduate at St John's.

In 1571 Jesus College came into being with Elizabeth as its titular founder. In point of fact the funds were provided by Doctor Price and from the start it became a predominantly Welsh college.

In 1598 Sir Thomas Bodley of Magdalen offered to replenish Duke Humphrey's library and by 1602 had collected over 2,000 volumes.

STUART AND JACOBITE OXFORD

Elizabeth had shown a strong affection for Oxford. Charles I used Christ Church as his H.Q. in the Civil War, keeping his Queen at Merton.

In James I's reign, in 1610, Nicholas Wadham and his wife began to build the college that bears their name on the site of the old Augustinian Convent just outside Smith Gate. It was intended for west country scholars as was only natural, seeing that they were natives of Branscombe in Devon. Robert Blake was one of the first undergraduates and Sir Walter Raleigh's son and General Monk's brother helped to keep up the west country tradition.

In 1624 with funds bequeathed by Thomas Tesdale (intended for Balliol) and Richard Wightwicke, Broadgates Hall was converted into Pembroke College, mainly famous for the fact that it later counted Samuel Johnson among its pupils. Professorships of Geometry, Astronomy, Philosophy, History and Music were added. Even Anatomy began to be studied.

Fashion was beginning to turn against the Calvinists and the High Church due in large measure to Laud, who in 1630 became Chancellor, became a powerful force. Laud was an ardent reformer and was at the zenith of his power when Charles I was entertained by him in 1636 in the magnificent new buildings that he had added to St John's. Laud's Code survived in Oxford even after Laud himself fell, so Charles brought his army to Oxford, and his Court to Christ Church. His ministers were lodged in other colleges. His courtiers played havoc with the college cellars and his Treasury demanded and got all the college plate except that at Corpus which has to be seen to be believed. It may easily be seen on application to the President. Undergraduates joined his army and dug fortifications, neglecting lectures to do so. When however in 1646 Charles fled from Oxford, his stock declined, and when Cromwell visited the University he was elected Chancellor.

Colleges were purged of 'malignants' and new professors and fellows appointed. The heads of all but three colleges were replaced. Among those to go were Doctor Samuel Fell, Dean of Christ Church. The supplanters were, unexpectedly perhaps, men of distinction and included Dean Owen of Christ Church, John Conant, Rector of Exeter and John Wilkins, President of Wadham. Wilkins in particular collected a remarkable group of scientific men including Robert Boyle, John Locke and Sir Christopher Wren.

At the Restoration Lord Clarendon came back as Chancellor, the Cavaliers re-established their old ascendancy and the standard of conduct relaxed. Charles II visited Oxford in 1663 and brought his Court there in 1665 to escape the Plague. Clarendon retired to France in 1667 to write his History and from its profits rose the Clarendon Printing House. Sheldon was Chancellor for a short time and left the Sheldonian theatre, built for him by Sir Christopher Wren, as a perpetual memorial.

John Fell, the son of Samuel, who had been an undergraduate of Christ Church when he was eleven, and later an ensign in the Royalist Army, returned as Dean of Christ Church in 1675 and crowned Tom Quad with Wren's Tower in addition to completing the college buildings. He was a man of character, for in addition to entertaining both Charles II and James II he expelled John Locke, patronized Anthony Wood, and refused to honour Titus Oates. Doctor Fell, whose statue stands above the archway leading from Tom Quad to Peckwater, is today remembered by vast numbers of people who know nothing whatever about him or Oxford, by four lines of doggerel:

> *I do not like thee Doctor Fell,*
> *The reason why I cannot tell,*
> *But this I know, and know full well,*
> *I do not like thee Doctor Fell.*

Perhaps, who knows, these lines were the work of John Locke.

The Ashmolean Museum was opened in 1683 to house the collections of rarities made by John Tradescant and Elias Ashmole.

James II mistakenly tried to convert Oxford to Catholicism by opening two Catholic chapels, but the opposition of the Magdalen dons was too strong for him.

There was nothing in the character of William of Orange to commend him to Oxford, beyond the fact that anybody would be a pleasant change after the egregious James, so it was with no small relief that Oxford welcomed the accession of Queen Anne, who was a special friend of the Church.

In 1710 the rally of the Tory Churchmen turned Dr Sacheverell of Magdalen (a foolish man) into a national hero and almost swept the Act of Settlement away.

But Hanoverian Oxford was composed partly of angry, disappointed Jacobites and Whigs who were not too happy about the future. Oxford suffered an eclipse. The Heads of Colleges drank too much and worked too little. Enthusiasm for anything was suspect. Only Party feelings ran high. The general tone was Tory with a few outbreaks of Jacobite fever. Gentlemen commoners began to increase in number rapidly, as did their expenses as William Pitt found at Trinity in 1727.

Professors were content to take their salary and give no lectures, with the result that Edmund Gibbon went down after fourteen months with no love for what he called his 'alma mater', Joseph Butler condemned Oxford studies as frivolous and tiresome and Bentham trounced the system with a Gibbon-like venom.

In spite of this there were brilliant men at Oxford in those days, among them Joseph Addison of Queen's who held his fellowship at Magdalen till 1711. Samuel Johnson came up to Pembroke in 1728 and Blackstone, a member of the same college, became one of the most famous of all Fellows of All Souls.

Adam Smith went up to Balliol in 1740 and Charles James Fox was a gentleman commoner of Hertford in 1764. John Wesley went up to Christ Church in 1720 and later as a fellow of Lincoln revived an enthusiasm for piety and devotion which caused the Methodists who followed him to be driven out of Oxford, an act which earned the commendation of Johnson who was himself an enthusiast of piety.

In this century Hawksmoor built the new Queen's College and the back quadrangle of All Souls. George Clarke, Doctor Woodroffe, and Sir George Cookes combined to build Worcester College on the site where the Gloucestershire monks had lived, and in 1739 Doctor Newton converted Hart Hall into Hertford.

MODERN OXFORD

At the end of the eighteenth century John Eveleigh, Provost of Oriel in 1781, Cyril Jackson, Dean of Christ Church in 1783 and John Parsons, Master of Balliol in 1798 combined to effect a reform and in 1800 a new Examination

Statute established both a Pass and an Honours Examination. Under Jackson, Christ Church, always the nursery of statesmen, began to soar. There was so great a competition to become a member of 'The House' that according to de Quincey, not even a dog-kennel was left untenanted. Jackson had an especial gift for managing 'that most unmanageable class of undergraduates, Noble-men'. The Dean made even dukes work. He was able even to make earls take an interest in Homer. He inspired Robert Peel to work like a tiger; after gaining a double First Peel was in the House of Commons within six months.

Christ Church had the singular honour of producing five prime ministers in a single century.

Balliol, too, recovered from a severe lapse in which its numbers had fallen from 192 to 75 in 1785 owing to the efforts of Dr Parsons. Copleston, Provost of Oriel in 1795, revived the fortunes of that college with such success that it became the centre of the religious and aesthetic movements of the following century.

Not that revolutionary ideas were encouraged as Walter Savage Landor at Trinity and Percy Bysshe Shelley at University College discovered to their cost.

When W. E. Gladstone followed Canning and Peel at Christ Church in 1828 the University like the city was not greatly altered in essentials from the old Oxford. Privilege and tradition were still all-important.

But between the time when Gladstone came up in 1828 and became Member for the University in 1847, the Oxford Movement had come into being and faded out again.

This strong revival of religious feeling was led by a very vigorous group of famous men.

In 1811 Thomas Arnold became a Scholar of Corpus, and John Keble a Fellow of Oriel. In 1822 J. H. Newman also became a Fellow of Oriel, as did E. B. Pusey in 1823, and Froude and Wilberforce in 1826. Henry Manning went up to Balliol in 1827, and Benjamin Jowett won a Balliol Scholarship in 1838. It was in 1828 that Newman began his famous sermons in St Mary's and in 1833 after Keble's sermon on National Apostasy the new crusade really began.

The Union Society was founded in 1829. Catholic Emancipation and Parliamentary Reform were at last carried, the Duke of Wellington became Chancellor and the Tractarian Movement was in full swing. From 1833 to 1845 religious controversy waxed ever more fiercely until one side took their stand with Keble and Pusey, and the others went over with Newman into the Church of Rome.

Then came the Liberal reaction, the attempt to abolish privileges for men of rank, at improving discipline, lowering expenditure, shaking up the dons into intellectual activity, the throwing open of fellowships and scholarships, the surrender of clerical control. By the Act of 1854, mainly owing to Gladstone, many of these reforms were adopted.

The professorial system was reorganized and partly endowed from college funds. Fellowships and scholarships were awarded on merit. Vested interests were abolished. In 1871 the University ceased to be the preserve of the Church of England.

The demand for a Science Museum, under the leadership of Dr Acland in 1845, began to be heard. John Ruskin came up to Oxford in 1837 and became Professor of Fine Arts in 1870. The Pre-Raphaelites began to beautify the world. In 1860 Bishop Wilberforce, challenging Darwin's theories, was answered by Professor Huxley, and Jowett made Balliol a training ground for statesmen, notable among whom were Asquith, Milner, Lord Curzon and Earl Grey. Liddell of the Greek Lexicon fame became Dean of Christ Church and became even more famous by reason of the stories told to his seven year old daughter Alice by the shy eccentric mathematical don, Dodgson, better known to the outside world as Lewis Carroll.

Liddell, however, was in addition to his Greek scholarship a great builder and did much to add to the architectural glories of 'The House'.

New College, Magdalen, University, Trinity and Corpus all came into the front of the picture. Balliol and Exeter were rebuilt and Sir Thomas Jackson created the new Examination Schools. Trinity and Brasenose added quadrangles.

Keble was founded in 1870 to preserve the memories of the Tractarians and Hereford was re-established by Thomas Baring in 1874.

All the old halls except St Edmund Hall were absorbed in the colleges and Nonconformist colleges came into existence, notably Mansfield in 1885. Women were at last admitted into the University and in 1879 two colleges, Somerville and Lady Margaret Hall, were built to house them.

In my day women undergraduates were regarded with marked disfavour. The modern undergraduate has come to regard them as a decided asset and with this judgment I agree.

Cecil Rhodes who was found unacceptable at University College came up to Oriel and became one of Oxford's most princely benefactors, founding scholarships for men from overseas which have resulted in a considerably higher standard of athletics if not of learning. Athletics have not of course

F

always occupied so prominent a place in the life of the undergraduate as they do today.

The first boat-race, between Brasenose and Jesus, took place in 1815. The first Inter-University Boat Race was rowed in 1829, but it did not become an annual fixture till 1856.

The first Oxford and Cambridge cricket match was played in 1827. The Inter-University football matches were not started till 1873.

New Schools came into being, notably that of English Language and Literature, which attracts vast numbers of young women today but in my time was regarded with disfavour by the authorities in spite of the impetus given to it by Sir Walter Raleigh, Modern Languages, History, Geography, Forestry and Engineering.

In 1907 Lord Curzon became Chancellor and advocated degrees for women and the abolition of compulsory Greek. Neither idea commended itself to the University authorities.

In 1914 the world of Oxford came to an abrupt if temporary finish. 14,500 members of the University went out to fight against Germany and extremely few of them returned alive.

In the interim between the wars Oxford grew to about 4,500, the number of women being fixed at not more than one quarter of the number of men.

This has had the result of making girls at school work so hard to get into Oxford that they overwork their intellectual strength and get the wrong idea about the value of study. Many of them got no value out of Oxford at all beyond a degree which means that they can avoid starvation by teaching.

The first woman to be given the title of Professor was granted that honour in 1945.

The Honours School of Philosophy, Politics, Economics, now the most popular of all, came into being in 1923, Geography followed in 1932, Agriculture in 1937 and Forestry in 1944.

Lord Nuffield gave a tremendous impetus to the study of medicine by endowing the medical school with two million pounds for research and experiment. He further founded in 1937 a college for the encouragement of social studies.

In 1939 the life of the University again stopped abruptly. On this occasion the Colleges were taken over by Government departments, most of the dons were given posts of responsibility in one or other of these Universities and the undergraduates as usual went off to fight.

On this occasion quite a large number came back, a number indeed so large as to embarrass the authorities, for there are now 6,000 undergraduates in evidence, though by now most of the ex-service men and their wives and children have gone down with their certificates to prove to the world that they are capable of doing jobs if any employer can find a job for them to do. So long as the Civil Service contains most of the able-bodied clerical workers in the country detailed to prevent the rest of the country from doing any work of their own there will presumably be jobs of a sort; but Oxford encourages initiative and original thinking almost as much as the present Government discourages those virtues.

The Oxford of today is a splendid place. It is only the thought of the hereafter which is apt, occasionally, to cloud the brow of the undergraduate.

CHAPTER IV

Architecture of Oxford

I KNOW no sight more pleasing to the eye and other senses than that of attractive young things in attractive old surroundings. Not all young things are attractive, not all old buildings pleasing. But on the whole Oxford does attract the most pleasant type of young man, a fair number of fair young women, and there is no question whatever that it contains among much that is execrable some of the loveliest buildings in the world. Accustomed to them as I am I never tire of the symmetry and magnificence of Tom Quad, the vaulted staircase to Christ Church Hall, Magdalen Tower, Mob Quad at Merton, the gardens backed by the City Wall of New College, the deer park at Magdalen, the cloisters of New College and Magdalen, or the gardens of Wadham, St John's, and Worcester.

And the beauty of all these is considerably enhanced by the presence of the young men and girls who infuse vitality into these stones.

Charles Lamb found delight in Oxford in Long Vacation. I don't. The delight that I take in Oxford depends on this combination of light, musical, if sometimes too drawlingly affected, voices, slim figures with shining hair and unlined faces and grey crumbling walls, pinnacles, turrets, spires and towers.

Colour, of course, makes a difference. Even Oxford is apt to be a dim place when wreathed in the wet white river mists of February.

In June when the blue of the delphiniums vies with the blue of the sky and reflects itself in the eyes of the beholders, Oxford is Arcadia.

The enthusiast for architecture in general will be particularly happy in Oxford, for it is not like Bath, Cheltenham and Tenby a homogeneous town of one period, but a palimpsest of layers of every period. Palladian and Gothic stand cheek by jowl with Transitional and Norman. You take your pick.

Oxford's buildings represent every century from the eleventh, though the colleges as you have already seen are of later date than the Norman. Only one college, Merton, and only one university building, the old Congregation House, have examples of an earlier style than the Perpendicular. Magdalen is the only college to possess an unaltered medieval quadrangle.

It is quite true that Oxford whispers from her towers the last enchantments of the Middle Ages. There is no other town in England in which the medieval styles can be studied with an equal wealth of illustration.

The streets of the city are almost exactly those of Anglo-Saxon Oxford, but the only survival of that period is the tower of St Michael's Church in the Cornmarket.

The main Norman work is the great mound that stands by the prison. This was the 'motte' of the castle built by Robert D'Oilgi, who represented William the Conqueror in Oxford. He replaced this 'motte' in 1071 by the stone tower that overlooks the river. Its walls are of tremendous thickness.

The best example of Norman architecture in Oxford is in the West Door of Iffley church, pleasantly reached by way of the towpath, unpleasantly reached by way of Iffley Road. The prevailing ornament here is the deeply cut chevron or zig-zag. There are also Norman arches in the delightful little church of St Peter-in-the-East in Queen's Lane, in St Aldates, St Ebbe's and Ferry Hinksey.

In the Cathedral you will see the finest example of the development of Gothic from Norman in the country. At the east end, begun about 1150, all the arches are round and massive, but as you look westward you will find the pointed Gothic arches prevailing. The magnificent vaulted ceiling is, of course, of later date.

In St Giles' church you will also find excellent examples of Early English Gothic, with a font decorated with pyramidal 'dog-tooth' work.

The steep pitched stone roofed Muniment Room in Mob Quad, Merton, dates from this period, as do the medieval 'mansiones' of Worcester.

The quadrangular plan did not gain general acceptance until New College adopted it in 1380.

The outstanding example of the Decorated style in Oxford is St Mary's Spire begun by Richard of Abingdon in 1275. This was followed in 1320 by the old Congregation House, the first building to be owned by the University as such.

The south aisle of St Mary Magdalene, which has exquisite buttresses, was built in 1337 and the west window added in 1360.

New College gave the lead in the Perpendicular style which was followed by All Souls in 1440, Magdalen in the latter part of the fifteenth century, while Merton Tower was finished in 1450. Stained glass was put in wherever possible, but it will doubtless surprise you to know that Oxford still possesses a richer store of medieval glass than any other English city except York. Particularly lovely is the glass in the ante-chapel of New College put in in 1386, the ante-chapel of All Souls inserted in 1442, and the heraldic sixteenth century glass in the library at Balliol and St Ebbe's church.

It is commonly accepted that the Divinity School which was completed about 1480 is the finest Perpendicular building in existence. Its vast windows occupy the whole of the space between the buttresses. The ceiling of the Divinity School, like that of the Cathedral choir which dates from about 1500, shows the progress made by ribbed vaulting since the building of the Latin Chapel in the mid-fourteenth century.

There is fan-vaulting in the porch of All Souls chapel which dates from 1442, but the most magnificent specimen is that of the Hall staircase at Christ Church which was not constructed till 1640.

It is in Wadham that the type of building most characteristic of the collegiate system can best be studied. Its date is 1613. The builders retained the medieval idea of grouping sets of rooms round a quadrangle, as the most convenient way of shutting out the world and shutting in the scholars. They kept also the traditional great gateway, a legacy of military architecture, flanked by a porter's lodge, with rooms above for the Warden to supervise all exits and entrances. They also copied the medieval arrangements for the chapel, but they abandoned tracery and the pointed arch and contented themselves with ornamenting the tower with external columns supporting not arches but lintels. We see this at St John's, Merton and in the Examination Schools. It is a principle of building that we see in Stonehenge.

Three types of columns were evolved. The earliest, the Doric, can be seen in the columns of Canterbury Gate at Christ Church; the next was the Ionic to be seen in the Ashmolean Museum, and the third was the Corinthian which can be seen in the columns of All Saints'.

These are, of course, imitations of the Roman versions of the Greek orders.

Perhaps the loveliest product of the seventeenth century is the inner quad with the Garden front of St John's. Louis XIV's Palladian palace at Versailles served Wren as a model for the garden quadrangle at Trinity and for that at New College.

Hawksmoor, a pupil of Wren, early in the eighteenth century constructed an almost perfect example of Palladian architecture in Queen's. Peckwater Quad, Christ Church, a most dignified, rich-looking affair that has recently been replaced, dates from 1705 and the Library immediately opposite which badly needs repairing from 1761.

New College modernized its front quad by the insertion of Palladian windows and adding an upper storey at the end of the seventeenth century.

Townesend built a fine Palladian block for Corpus on its Meadow Front in 1706 and Balliol added the Fisher Buildings in 1769.

The outstanding example, however, of Palladian architecture in Oxford is undoubtedly the Radcliffe Camera, built by James Gibbs in 1749.

With the nineteenth century came Sir Gilbert Scott and the revival of an interest in Gothic. Hence the Martyrs' Memorial designed in imitation of the Eleanor crosses of 1291.

Unfortunately each architect soon gave up direct imitation and began to give his own version of the Gothic. One example of this is to be seen in Exeter, the chapel of which is a close imitation of the Sainte Chapelle, but the Broad Street front (1856) is all Scott's own, as is the Holywell front of New College put up in 1876. Then came Butterfield with his catastrophic Victorian Gulliver's box of bricks in 1870 and the result was the nadir that is Keble.

To Ruskin goes the discredit of the University Museum put up in 1860 by Sir Thomas Deane under his influence. Deane was also responsible for the hideous Meadow Buildings of Christ Church (1862).

Modern Balliol is the work of Mr Waterhouse, and Sir Charles Barry, architect of the Houses of Parliament, was responsible for the western block of the High Street front of University college (1843).

St Swithin's Quad, Magdalen, was built by Mr Bodley in the 1880s and if it does not add lustre to the lovely ancient buildings of that exquisitely beautiful college, it does at least not disgrace them.

Mansfield College, built by Mr Champneys in 1889, also proves that it was possible to build gracefully even in the late Victorian era.

As you will see from this short summary it is possible in a short walk to recognize the styles of every century from the Norman period to our own, the latest addition being the New Bodleian and the Laboratories.

Oxford is singularly lucky in respect of the fact that almost until living memory she remained in appearance a medieval city.

She had and still has a wealth of gardens in which her buildings were set like gems. This was due to the fact that the monks required a certain amount of garden for privacy and exercise in each of their hostels, and at the Dissolution these gardens were seized by the founders of colleges. Wolsey, for instance, came into possession of St Frideswide's and Stockwell Meads and laid out the Broad Walk in Christ Church Meadows. St John's inherited the garden of St Bernard's College, and its famous gardens were laid out by Capability Brown. Dorothy Wadham acquired the grounds of the House of Austin Friars, but part of this has recently been sold to the Rhodes Trust.

New College owes its spacious grounds partly to the depopulation of the city following the Black Death, and partly to the fact that William of Wykeham bought land from the Trinitarian Friars. The magnificent screen of wrought iron that faces the gardens of New College came from the palace of the first Duke of Chandos.

Magdalen Grove once belonged to the Hospital of St John the Baptist. The deer are the descendants of those brought from the park of the Bishop of Winchester and as they are 'on the foundation' the college does not eat them.

Merton owes its garden to the enclosure of the pomerium and Corpus acquired its gardens from Merton.

The purpose of college gardens in the Middle Ages was mainly for the provision of fruit and herbs. The Botanic Gardens are the only ones that remain to represent the ideals prevailing at the time of their lay-out.

No visitor should leave Oxford before getting some idea of the individual architecture of each college, but after doing this he will immensely enhance the memorableness of his impression if he climbs up Boar's Hill or to Elsfield and looks down on the whole city, for the ensemble of spires and towers seen from above is one of the wonders of the world.

Magdalen College

The Front Quadrangle, Corpus Christi College

The Front Quadrangle, St John's College

The Quadrangle, St Edmund Hall

CHAPTER V

The Oxford of the Undergraduate

MY father taught me to skate by the simple but brutal method of leading me to the middle of a frozen dam and leaving me to find my way to the edge as best I could.

When I was an undergraduate the system was to provide each freshman with a Book of Statutes that were written in Latin and leave him to discover his way about by himself.

It took me more than four years. I made many mistakes. I did too little work, spent far too much money, took a great deal of unnecessary exercise, and omitted to join either the Union or the O.U.D.S., two of the most worthwhile societies in the University.

The object of Oxford is to teach a young man how to live, how to get on with all sorts of other men (and women), and how to think.

I resented a good deal of my early days at Oxford. I could not get used to the enervating damp climate. I was for ever catching cold, and always inclined to go to sleep. I even used to go to sleep between tea and dinner. I was always disinclined to work. I resented most of all the curtailment of my liberty and the fact that I could not leave college after 9.20 at night. I used to make a habit of going out into the streets at 9.15 and walking aimlessly about for an hour or so. This was at times not unexciting because the streets were patrolled by a proctor (don in cap and gown) accompanied by two bull-dogs (porters in bowler hats and gym shoes) whose office it was to chase any undergraduate seen without cap and gown, bring him back to the proctor who would then say 'Your name and College, Sir?'

For this misdemeanour the culprit had to appear at the proctor's office the following morning at 10 o'clock and pay a fine of 6s 8d.

If you were caught in a pub (not one of my habits) or talking to a girl (one of my habits) the disciplinary measures taken were more severe. To avoid this I used to talk and walk with my girl along the tow-path which was not a resort of the proctors. I wasted many thousands of invaluable hours in this insipid way learning nothing. I ought to have been reading or listening or talking or acting. There were of course no cinemas and there was no wireless. I didn't drink partly because I couldn't afford it, but mainly because I was in strict training, first for Rugger and later for running.

Each Sunday I used to leave Oxford either by train for Didcot in order to walk over the Berkshire Downs to the White Horse Hill above Uffington, or to Banbury in order to walk out past Broughton Castle to Edgehill and Moreton-in-Marsh, where I caught the evening train home. Sometimes I would walk up the valley of the Windrush or Evenlode, read the lessons for some country rector and wander back later at night. This met with the disapproval of my Dean who accused me of disloyalty to my college in failing to attend Matins in Cathedral. He was slightly mollified when I told him about my lesson-reading.

It seems hard to believe today, but in those days it was the practice of members of the House to perambulate the Parks on Sunday afternoons in dark suits and bowler hats. There was also at 9.15 a weekly Sunday concert in Balliol open to the whole University.

In the summer term we spent many of our afternoons and evenings lying in punts moored up under the shade of the willows on the Cher, pretending to work, but usually asleep. This practice still holds except that the present-day undergraduate is usually accompanied by a fair partner, which in my time would have led to questions and undoubted trouble.

I did most of my reading in Blackwell's, browsing over new books that I couldn't afford to buy but found very much more to my liking than the mathematical text books that I couldn't even pretend to understand. Among my other mistakes was the selection of Mathematics as a School for Honour Moderations. I had taken Classics at school and if I had had any sense at all I should have taken Greats.

I got a third class in Moderations after two years, and after two more years got a further third in the Final Honours School of English Language and Literature which I found much more palatable even if I failed to improve my class in it. I am now convinced that for any young man of ability there is only one School to take at Oxford, and that is 'Greats'.

The man who takes a 'first' in 'Greats' is always capable of securing and holding down jobs of responsibility. A training in the Classics has the faculty of making a man malleable and adaptable to almost any conditions.

Pure mathematics are of no value commercially or socially. English is a fine leisure-hour accomplishment for the aesthete, but the odd thing is that the average 'Greats' man knows more English than the man who has specialized in English.

Today the normal School for the short-course man to take is 'P.P.E.' which is short for Politics, Philosophy and Economics, though how any man can expect to acquire more than a smattering of any one of these in two years I don't know.

History used to be the most popular School for those seeking Honours, but in my time, in a less hurried world of less competitors the majority of undergraduates were content to read for a Pass Degree which was an euphemism for doing no work at all and enjoying a weekly genial chatter with a Tutor who was certainly relieved if you failed to produce an essay.

Attendance at lectures was, and I believe still is, voluntary. I have always been addicted to lectures and I went to lectures by Hadow on Aristotle, Mackail on Dante and Carlyle on the Old Testament, subjects which had little to do with Mathematics.

Lectures are much better attended today than they used to be. All women are lecture-minded and most present-day undergraduates have one aim only, to get a degree as quickly as possible and make sure of a living wage.

In my time the House library was little used. I never once entered it during the whole of my four years in residence. The Bodleian and Radcliffe Camera were always half-empty. Today there is a long queue outside both these libraries before 9 a.m., when it opens, and 2 p.m., when it re-opens. There is never enough room to sit down and it often takes two days to get a book. One reason for this is the greatly increased number of undergraduates, another is the general shortage of text books, so that you can't buy your text books even if you can afford them; and it has to be remembered that in spite of Service grants, State scholarships and other Government aids the majority of undergraduates are poor. In my day Oxford was a place of immense wealth. Did not the Gaekwar of Baroda, Sir Philip Sassoon, and Sir James Horlick share my staircase?

The majority of undergraduates today come from State-aided schools in the north, and are drawn from the lower middle classes.

That perhaps explains in some measure why we were left to find our own level, sink and swim, while the present-day undergraduate is regimented, spoon-fed and bedroomed as if he were on a Cook's Tour.

It is symptomatic of the times that for the first time in the whole history of Oxford there has just been published a guide specially written for undergraduates bearing the title *Oxford University. What's What.*

It is a very useful guide indeed and told me a good deal that in spite of my forty years' experience I did not know before. It begins with a tour round the University which no undergraduate of my time ever undertook.

I would here enter the caveat that to try to see all the twenty-eight colleges in a single day is folly and a waste of strength and time. If you have only a day in which to see Oxford, content yourself with Christ Church, the richest, the noblest and the largest, Merton (in my opinion the oldest) and Magdalen, by far the most beautiful.

The Editor of *What's What*, John Widdicombe, solves the problem of which is the oldest college by reminding us that University was the first to be endowed (1249), Balliol had the first fixed locality (1260) and Merton the earliest statues (1264). 'All', he says, 'are certainly earlier than any Cambridge college.'

Undergraduates at University College, which expelled Shelley after two terms and now exhibits an execrable statue of him lying drowned looking like a piece of cod on a fishmonger's slab, claim that their college was founded by Alfred the Great. This has about as much foundation in fact as the story of his burning the cakes at Athelney.

I did not know before that the Queen's College, Oxford and Queens' College, Cambridge – note the all-important positions of the apostrophes – share a common crest, the boar's head. The Queen's College which recruits mainly from the north country and summons its members to dinner by means of trumpets, was founded on behalf of Philippa, wife of Edward III, and is a hundred years older than Queens' College, Cambridge.

Just opposite Queen's, in Queen's Lane, stands the lovely but small and unpretentious St Edmund's Hall, a remarkable example of the changes of fortune that overtake colleges within a generation. In my time scarcely anybody knew of its existence. Today it holds the record for producing more Blues and more 'Firsts' than any other college of whatever size.

New College, which is never abbreviated to 'New', is the natural resort of Old Wykehamists as both the school and college were founded by William of Wykeham. It is remarkable for its cloisters, stained-glass and the Warden in my time, Spooner, who was the originator of the word 'spoonerism'. He is credited with having said to an undergraduate, 'You have tasted your worm, you have hissed my mystery lectures, and you must leave by the first town drain.' I myself heard him give out the hymn 'Kinkering Kongs their titles take'. I have a feeling, but cannot adduce facts to prove it, that having made a few, very few spoonerisms by accident and achieved a reputation for this oddity of speech Spooner played up to it.

The point is not so trivial as it might at first appear. A great number of Spoonerisms are the invention of later wags, like the famous 'Will you take me?' supposed to have been said in all innocence to the lady who said 'Yes' and so became Mrs Spooner. But Senior Common Room is a peculiar institution. Masters' Common Rooms in Public Schools breed oddities, but they have nothing on the Senior Common Rooms of Oxford Colleges, where ageing scholars can indulge idiosyncrasies that would be severely discouraged in the home. Men with abnormal brains develop abnormality in dress, speech and even decorum, and college life is the richer for dons whose behaviour is not moulded by convention nor obeys the unwritten laws of the Civil Service.

Doctor Johnson was right when he described dining with the Canons of Christ Church as one of life's rarest privileges, and conversation at High Table for those of us who don't belong to it is both dazzling and memorable. Men whose lives are spent in the rarified aura of philosophy or some esoteric science are a law unto themselves, and there is no question that most of them cultivate curious manners and build up for themselves reputations for wearing too few clothes or too many partly for their own convenience and partly to establish their personalities.

Spooner did not rely wholly on Spoonerisms. He was supposed to have a curious limit of vision which enabled irreverent undergraduates to cavort and pirouette round him as they entered his study, and even to cock a snoot at him until they came within a few feet when they would assume the conventional air of the pupil. He told me years after I had gone down that he saw my earlier antics and enjoyed them.

The point that I would make here is that you cannot pretend to have seen Oxford until you have not only penetrated the arcana of an undergraduate's room, which is easy, but also enjoyed the port and snuff that are the aftermath of every High Table dinner in Hall, access to which ought not to be impossible now that so many dons have yielded to the lure of the Government to take part in public life.

This digression you may remember took place in New College, whose front gate is hidden in a lane that leads by way of the Bridge of Sighs to Hertford, a curious college which went bankrupt in the eighteenth century and was inhabited by squatters.

Among its more famous squatters in our own time was Evelyn Waugh.

Opposite Hertford there is a confused jumble of University buildings the architecture of which may displease, but the importance of which should not fail to interest you.

In one, the old Clarendon, is the spider's web of the Proctor. This was formerly the Clarendon Press which was moved to Walton Street in 1830. Behind it stands the Sheldonian, a circular rather dim building, designed by

Sir Christopher Wren, in which all Degrees are conferred and concerts held.

Convocation, or the Ceremony of Degree-giving is an elaborate, lengthy but colourful ritual, involving a good deal of speech-making in Latin and much kneeling and praying. It is the door by which we leave the University proudly dressed in the long gown and white rabbit-fur hood of Bachelor of Arts, borrowed for the day from one's scout at the profitable fee of one guinea. Three years later we are at liberty to return if we have enough money, and by virtue of paying twelve guineas without further examination be further glorified by the substitution of the even longer gown and scarlet satin hood of the Master of Arts, also borrowed for the same fee. There is a curious superstition that the M.A. is somehow more highly gifted intellectually than the B.A. This is not the case. He is merely older. London University takes the more natural line of expecting a wider application of learning before conferring a Mastership on the Bachelor.

Doctors of any subject wear more resplendent robes, and many Doctorates, notably that of Civil Law, are conferred upon those whom the University delights to honour for victories won on the field of battle or commerce. Rich benefactors, explorers, scientists, even prominent politicians who may be wholly ignorant of the law are often made Honorary Doctors of Civil Law. What those lawyers who have won this distinction by pure learning think about all this is not known.

The old Bodleian Library, a lovely building both outside and in stands close by the Sheldonian.

The Bodleian is one of the few libraries in the British Isles (Trinity College, Dublin, the British Museum and the University Library of Wales at Aberystwyth are others), which has the right to a copy of every book that is printed in the British Isles. This explains the necessity for the miles of hecatombs that run under the Broad, corridors piled high with bookshelves that connect the old Bodleian with the new. The Bodleian was founded by Duke Humphrey. It takes its name from Sir Thomas Bodley who restored it in 1602.

Books are loaned, solely on condition that they are read on the premises. Charles I was severely rebuked for daring to ask for permission to have one sent to him to read when he was in residence at Christ Church during the Civil War. Present day undergraduates do not exhibit a like folly, they merely purloin them. If they are discovered they are not permitted to return. In my day the Bodleian was frequented only by foreigners and dons. Today it is the rendezvous of all the most attractive young women from Lady Margaret Hall and Somerville who distract most make undergraduates from the study of the old and tedious to a far more concentrated study of the young and disturbing.

Nothing is said on the reader's ticket about the purpose of one's visit to the library.

The Radcliffe Camera, a testing-ground for nocturnal climbers, is by day used as an annex to the Bodleian. The reading tables are commodious, the chairs comfortable. Those who are not in search of their Egeria often use the reading-room for their post-prandial siesta. There is no law about keeping awake.

Cheek by jowl with the Bodleian is the Divinity School, which in Henry VIII's time was the pig market.

In the narrow street close by (the Turl) are many shops and three colleges. Exeter, the chapel of which contains Pre-Raphaelite tapestries woven by William Morris and Burne-Jones, who were members of this College, Lincoln which has no special claim to fame, and Jesus, once the College where T. E. Lawrence hid himself unobtrusively for four years when he wasn't rubbing brasses or exploring the city sewers in a canoe, the home of all Welshmen as Exeter is the home of most West Countrymen.

On St David's Day the patriotic Welshmen hoist a bunch of leeks on the top of their flag-pole, an act which regularly causes the equally patriotic members of Exeter to haul it down again.

Local feuds between individual colleges are long-standing. Balliol and Trinity seize every excuse, notably that of Torpids and Eights, to raid each other. Magdalen and the House occasionally sally forth in pursuit of each other, and when T. E. Lawrence returned as a Fellow of All Souls he engineered a raid on the deer that are kept in Magdalen Grove, but this was one of the few raids planned by this intrepid spirit that failed.

Trinity which faces the Broad on its Northern side attracts a wide variety of undergraduates by reason of the excellence of its cellars. As it is often Head of the River, would-be Rowing Blues also clamour for admittance.

Balliol, the ugliest of all colleges bar one, was founded by John of Balliol as a penance for insulting a bishop. It has a reputation for being unusually erudite, which is no more deserved than its reputation for being wholly black. It is true that it attracts the coloured races and it is true that it housed in the past many notable scholars, but it is mainly remembered now for its famous Master, Doctor Jowett, who excelled all other dons, even Doctor Fell, for his sergeant-major-like tactics with undergraduates.

Just opposite Balliol at the entrance to St Giles stands the Martyrs' Memorial erected to the memory of Ridley, Latimer and Cranmer who were burnt at the stake here.

Adjoining Balliol on the north side is St John's (never alluded to as John's like its sister college in Cambridge), a large college with magnificent gardens, that are as quiet as they are colourful.

Living in Oxford is worth while if only for this ever-open escape from the turmoil of the streets. Here at any rate you catch the atmosphere of a University that is elsewhere apt to elude you.

At the far end of Beaumont Street which contains in the Randolph one of the ugliest hotels in the world, and in the Playhouse the most enterprising Repertory Company in Britain, stands Worcester, which contains a row of medieval 'mansions' formerly inhabited by members of the Benedictine Order and extensive gardens that contain a lake.

On the east side of St John's stands the newest and ugliest college, Keble, whose exterior looks like a Fair Isle sweater, once almost confined to under-graduates who intended to take Holy Orders. It used to be cheaper than the other colleges, and undergraduates used to mess together in Hall for all meals, which struck those of us who belonged to a different order as a most undesirable proceeding. Today communal feeding at breakfast and luncheon as well as at dinners has become the general rule.

Forty years ago at the House our scout would call us at whatever hour we desired, pour out the water into our hip bath, take our order for breakfast which generally included kedgeree, kippers, a couple of fried eggs and bacon, a pot of Cooper's marmalade and honey in the comb.

This meal we ate before a roaring fire alone in the seclusion of our own rooms. We had luncheon in the same royal solitary state and were at liberty to order almost anything from venison to grouse, salmon to fillet of steak, accompanied, of course, by the world-famous Christ Church meringues which were so plentiful that every visitor to the kitchen was given one.

For tea, also eaten in one's own rooms, there was no limit imposed on the number of muffins, crumpets, toasted tea cake or patisseries that we ordered.

Only for dinner at 7 o'clock were we expected to put on a gown and cross the quadrangle to the noble Dining Hall which is the largest but one in Britain. The largest is Westminster Hall. In that vast building dimly lit by candles on each table and two enormous log fires we enjoyed a four course dinner for which we were charged 1s 10d. Bread and napkins cost one penny apiece extra. I soon learned to do without either of these unessentials.

We Commoners who paid full fees, about £300 a year, sat below the salt in small groups of eight or ten.

Above the fireplace stood the lectern, from which a Scholar nightly gabbled off the Long Latin Grace. The Scholars, wearing longer gowns than

The Divinity School

The Front Quad, Oriel College

The High from Queen's Lane Corner

The Entrance Tower and Quadrangle, Wadham College

ours, sat by themselves at long tables immediately below the dais where sat the Fellows and Canons of Christ Church in evening dress.

There was a side-table where undergraduates entertained male guests.

We were expected to be in time for Grace, but we were at liberty to leave the hall when we had finished, for our meal took us much less time than the more sumptuous dinner provided at High Table. I suppose there were and are dons who work after dinner, but the lure of port and the conversation in Senior Common Room after this heavy meal must be hard to resist.

We of the lower orders commonly made our way to Junior Common Room for coffee and port and then dispersed to a Club meeting, more drinking in our rooms, the theatre, in pursuit of the other sex, or far less frequently in pursuit of learning.

It was a good life.

I was led into this digression by reason of Keble, which has one advantage over all the other colleges. It faces the University Parks, perhaps the most delectable place in Oxford. These Parks which are bordered on the east by the willow-fringed Cher are the haunt of nursemaids, small children and perambulators, but these can be avoided.

It is also the haunt of the Oxford University cricket eleven, and I for one would rather spend my early summer days surrounded by these tall swaying poplars, budding chestnut trees and mahogany coloured copper beeches than in any other place in the world. Here at any rate there is no pretence of work. Hatless undergraduates stand round the roped-off boundary and shining haired girls lie on their stomachs with their chins cupped in their hands watching the finest cricket in the world, that of first class county standards without first-class county championship seriousness. The fielders are more on their toes, the runners between the wickets swifter, the batsmen more enterprising than on any other ground I know, and there is nothing to mar either the symmetry of the colour or the quietude of the scene, for there is no noise of traffic and nothing to see beyond a world of green grass and green trees below and blue sky above. Here the birds sing merrily and the whole world is young, wearing its fresh summery look and there is nothing more serious in life than the fall of a wicket or the remote possibility of rain. Oxford may have many faults, but in the Parks when the Dark Blues are in the field it is compact of all the virtues, and life is both eternal and Elysian.

Only the very rich or the unwary, I may say in passing, indulge in the luxury of a deck-chair. The loan of these costs not tuppence but eighteen pence. Dons bring camp-stools, a thermos and a packet of sandwiches, the omniscient stand

H

just at the edge of the screen to watch the swing and the spin. The rest of us whose interest is evenly divided between the passing pageantry of perambulating youth and the players on the field stand a little back among the buttercups and hope that the day will never end.

When at last stumps are drawn we join the long procession past the University Museum, the Laboratores and the expensive Rhodes House, past Wadham, built in the golden age of architecture in imitation of a Tudor Manor house, to fall into the King's Arms for a pint and gossip before returning shall we say to Magdalen, the beauty of whose cloisters, Deer Park and Addison's Walk compensates in large measure for the end of cricket.

Magdalen was the college for 14 months of Gibbon who disliked it, and for some years of the Duke of Windsor who liked it very much and was himself very much liked. Addison, an undergraduate of Queen's, became a don at Magdalen. Prince Rupert. of the Rhine returned to it to house his big guns in the Civil War. In our own time Compton Mackenzie turned his knowledge of it to good account in *Sinister Street*, and Old Etonians of all generations naturally gravitate to it as it was founded by William Waynflete, the founder of Eton.

You may still see Oscar Wilde's ghost there, and one of the many gargoyles round the cloisters is said to resemble a famous Doctor Ellerton who ordered it to be defaced and scarified. In extreme age he was horrified to find that he had grown again to resemble the statue.

On May Day morning at dawn the choir boys of Magdalen climb the 150 ft high tower which was built in the year that Christopher Columbus crossed the Atlantic (1492) after having their trouser-pockets tapped to see that they do not contain eggs to hurl down on the pious listeners below, and from the roof sing ancient carols in the snow. The effect on their health is said to be deleterious, the effect on their voices is excellent, for they continue to sing like angels the whole year through as every listener-in to the wireless knows.

On the further side of the High below Magdalen Tower are the Botanical Gardens, famous for many exotic flowers and shrubs which grow out of soil that contains the dust of the medieval Jews who were not allowed to be buried within the city walls.

When finally you stand on the platform of the hideous station waiting for your homeward-bound train you may perhaps gain some crumb of comfort from the knowledge that you are standing on the site of the once beautiful Abbeys of Osney and Rewley.

CHAPTER VI

The Lighter Side of Oxford

THE Ashmolean Art Museum is exactly opposite the Randolph Hotel and well repays a visit. It contains the Ruskin collection of drawing and prints and in the painting section the paintings by Rubens, Van Dyke and Watteau as well as the early Italians. There are also periodical exhibitions of Contemporary Arts.

There are too many statues and some fine mummies, particularly in the Carnarvon section.

The University Art Club was founded in 1945.

There are two theatres, the New, a very splendid building opened in 1933 where West End Companies try out plays before opening in London, and the Playhouse, opened in 1923, where an excellent Repertory Company ring the changes on every type of play from Tchekov to *Charley's Aunt,* from *Hamlet* to Pantomime.

The University boasts two main dramatic societies, the O.U.D.S., founded in 1884, which gives two or three performances each year, and the Experimental Theatre Company which is of comparatively recent origin and puts on two plays a year. Each of these clubs boasts about a hundred members.

Every college has one or more dramatic societies, in addition to play-reading societies.

There are six cinemas in Oxford, four of them on the A.B.C. circuit. The Scala shows Continental films.

There are two film societies, the University Film Society which shows four films a term to 500 members and the Oxford Film Society which holds meetings on alternate Sunday nights during term time.

There is a long waiting list for membership of the many musical societies. The best known are the Eglesfield Players (Queen's), the Worcester and Somerville Musical Society, the St John's Madrigal Society, the Oxford University Musical Club and Union, the Bach Choir, the Bandits' Club Dance Orchestra, the Discord Club, and Harmonic Society, the Opera Club and the Oxford Orchestral Society. First-rate concerts are frequently held in the Sheldonian and every Sunday night in Balliol.

Attendance at dances outside college is banned, but the annual 'Commem' Balls, held in mid-June are probably the best run Balls in the world. Tickets are from four to six guineas a head inclusive of champagne supper. Special marquees are erected and the best known dance bands engaged. Each college holds a 'Commem' Ball about once every four years which means that there are six or seven held during 'Commem' week and all the tickets are snapped up on the day of issue as they must necessarily be limited to about 800 for each college.

These Balls begin at 10 p.m. and continue till dawn when breakfast is provided, and young couples in full evening dress may be seen patrolling the Broad or in punts on the river as late as midday all through the week.

'Commem' sees Oxford at its gayest and most care-free, for Schools are over, the Long Vacation has begun and the weather is nearly always fine.

Sport occupies a large proportion of the average undergraduates thought and time. Indeed to judge from the conversation in Vincent's Club, which consists almost exclusively of Blues, sport occupies practically all some undergraduates' thought and time.

To represent Oxford against Cambridge is somewhat naturally every healthy-bodied undergraduate's aim. The standard is high, so it is not surprising to find among Oxford undergraduates the amateur golf champion of the day, cricketers who play for first class counties and even in Test matches, and Rugby football players who represent their country. There is almost unlimited scope in Oxford for the player of every game and every type of sportsman.

Undergraduates run with the combined Christ Church, Magdalen and New College Beagles, ride to hounds with the Heythrop, V.W.H. (Cricklade), Bicester, South Oxfordshire, Old Berkeley, North Cotswold, and Duke of Beaufort's; play lawn tennis, real tennis, both codes of football, hockey, squash and fives. They also box and fence.

The most popular pursuit is rowing. Many colleges enter three or four crews for the Torpids in March, and for the Eights in May.

Athletes use the University Athletic Club track on the Iffley Road, or run across country with the Hare and Hounds Club.

Colleges, of course, play each other and the main Public Schools and the University teams play the most famous teams in the British Isles in preparation for their ordeal against Cambridge. Only those who actually play against Cambridge are awarded Blues, half Blues for the less exacting sports like chess, and full Blues for the major sports, like rowing, cricket, football, hockey, lawn tennis and golf and the first strings in the athletic events.

As there are so many crews on the narrow river, the colleges row in four divisions, in single file, each boat starting a length behind the one in front. If a college succeeds in catching up with, i.e. 'bumping' the eight in front, the crews change places on the following day. These races occupy the afternoons for a whole week, so that the crew which holds or gains its position at the Head of the River usually deserves the Bumper Supper which celebrates its triumph.

Cambridge has a slightly better record than Oxford over the years in most sports except Rugger where Oxford still holds the lead, but spectators can count on a fierce encounter in which no quarter is given on either side in any Inter-University contest.

The most thrilling of these contests is the Rugger match which yearly draws immense crowds to Twickenham.

Indeed the Rugby Football Club is financially responsible for many of the other clubs, notably the Cricket Club, for by an odd regulation the Cricket Club is not allowed to charge any entrance fee to the Parks in which they play all its home matches.

The women's colleges also indulge in hockey, lacrosse, tennis and even row not only against each other, but also against Cambridge

Among other sporting clubs are the Badminton, basket-ball, rifle, ski, table-tennis and yacht clubs. There is really no physical activity which is not catered for by one or other of the clubs and notices of these activities are posted in the lodge of each college, while all the more enterprising secretaries busily solicit the patronage of all freshmen within a week of their arrival.

It is considered part of the ordinary routine duty of every able-bodied undergraduate to represent his college in some department of sport, though no penalty attaches to those who prefer to roam over the hills by themselves or sit in their rooms and work all day.

The mornings are usually divided between attendance at lectures and the drinking of coffee in cafés usually in the society of a girl from one of the women's colleges.

In the evening either before or after dinner you will find undergraduates of both sexes occupying the bars of the more popular hotels and public houses.

Oxford is well equipped in the number and quality of her inns. There are well over a hundred within an easy walk of any college, and three hundred within an easy cycle ride.

The most popular at the moment are the King's Arms (the resort of the athletic), the Randolph (the haunt of the aesthetes), the Mitre, the Chequers, the Gloucester Arms, the Welsh Pony, the Horse and Jockey, the Royal Oak, the Lamb and Flag, the Eastgate, White's, the George, the Trout at Godstow especially on Sundays, the Marlborough Arms and the Bear at Woodstock and the Rose Revived at Newbridge.

All these are out of bounds to undergraduates, and all are well patronized by undergraduates.

All meals in college these days are taken, as I said, in Hall, but few are capable of satisfying the needs of the hard worker or strenuous athlete, so you will find overflow meetings of undergraduates in all the British Restaurants, the Angel, Cadena, Elliston's, the Forum, Fuller's, Golden Kettle, the Kemp, Long John's, the George, the Stowaway, Town and Gown, White's, Taj Mahal, and Welsh Pony, some of which cater only for tea, others for luncheon and dinner. The George is allowed to make a special house charge.

In order to get the best out of Oxford it is advisable for the undergraduate to be gregarious, for Oxford is after all in essence a network of clubs. There are some two hundred clubs and societies open to members of the University, apart altogether from the College Clubs, Old Boys' Societies, dining clubs and so on. I have only space to mention a few to show the extraordinary variety of interests that are catered for.

There is an Air Squadron founded in 1925 which gives full flying training to undergraduates.

The Bath Club is reserved for those male members of the University who have 'bathed within a women's college'. There used to be a tie for this club with silver embroidered taps or gold emblems if the members had left in possession of the bathroom taps.

The Bullingdon Club was founded in 1780 as a cricket club but it is now mainly composed of hunting men. The club is limited to thirty members. They dine in a barn. In my day they played an annual cricket match against the Athenaeum Club at Cambridge and full bottles of champagne were posted behind the wickets.

The Canning, Chatham, and Carlton Clubs are for Conservative undergraduates. There are political clubs for undergraduates of other political faiths.

There is an Oxford flotilla of the R.N.V.R.

The Gridiron Club founded in 1884 by the late Lord Salisbury is a social club of great distinction. There are now about sixty members.

Mathematicians join the Invariant Society and lawyers usually join the Blackstone or Law Society.

The Old Maids' Club is a women's club founded in 1948 with the avowed purpose of lowering the intellectual level of the University. This is achieved by playing 'ridiculous games with the most serious-minded and pompous clubs of the University'. A treasure hunt with the Bullingdon has taken place and tiddleywinks, spillikins and old maid are on the present agenda.

The Oxford Society which has a membership of 13,000 aims at uniting Oxford men and women.

There is a Railway Society which after 30 years is still flourishing, a Spectator Club for the non-specialist, the Union Debating Society which practically everybody joins for the sake of the dining room and library if not for the debates, and a Club for almost all the races and sects in the Universe.

Finally there is a wide selection of periodicals that provide the news and gossip of the week.

The oldest and most readable of these is the 'Isis' which is light and sometimes scurrilous. The 'Cherwell' is literary, the Oxford Magazine serious and inclined to be pompous, the Oxford Gazette publishes official lists and the 'Viewpoint' appears irregularly.

CHAPTER VII

Oxford University

THERE is an excellent *Handbook to the University of Oxford* published at 7s 6d by the Oxford University Press which no undergraduate ever reads, and few members of the public ever see because it is almost always out of print, but there are certain facts that you must know if you are to understand how Oxford works.

The maintenance of order rather than the spread of learning seems to have been the main consideration of the earliest authorities.

The hub of the University before the fourteenth century was St Mary's Church. There were a few colleges, Merton, Balliol, and University College, but these were far outnumbered by the residential halls and boarding houses.

The colleges looked after the accommodation, feeding and general welfare of the students and were responsible for the tutorial system, leaving to the University the supervision of all non-tutorial teaching, the libraries and museums and the control of degree-giving, examinations and regulation of finance. This division of responsibility still continues, the colleges remaining self-contained units, providing certain lectures open to the whole University and contributing to what is known as the University Chest.

It is advisable at this stage to get to know the meanings of some of the terms used in the University.

There is, first, Congregation, an assembly of about 800 holders of degrees who are responsible for the teaching. This body considers all decrees and statutes and passes them if the majority for the change is two-thirds. If it is less the proposed changes in the constitution must be submitted to Convocation, which consists of all University members who hold an M.A. or higher degree. There are about a thousand of these.

Convocation considers financial reports and is the only body possessed of the authority to fix the University Seal on legal documents. Its main duty however is to confer honorary degrees, and elect the Chancellor.

Convocation cannot of itself initiate measures. This is the work of the Hebdomadal Council which is a sort of Cabinet, containing twenty-three members, eighteen of whom are elected by Congregation, the remaining members being the Vice-Chancellor, Proctors and the last or next Vice-Chancellor.

The Chancellor (Lord Halifax) is a permanent member, but he seldom attends.

The Hebdomadal Council really runs the University, subject to the approval of Congregation who can compel the Council to bring in a measure by passing a resolution proposed by twelve members and supported by forty more.

The curators of the University Chest are responsible for finance.

In the Pope's Charter of 1218 annual tribute was levied on the town by the University and stored in an oak chest. Hence the name.

There is, in addition, a General Board of the Faculties which controls the fourteen Faculty Boards. There are eight Regius Professors appointed by the Crown. The rest are elected by special boards.

The Head of the University, the Chancellor, only visits Oxford on an invitation from the Vice-Chancellor who is chosen from the heads of the colleges and reappointed annually. He usually holds office for three years. The Chancellor holds office for life.

Each year two proctors are elected by the colleges in rotation. The permanent staff includes the Registrar who acts as Secretary to the Council, Congregation and Convocation.

There are also four deputy or pro-proctors who are responsible for the discipline both of undergraduates and B.A's. They have the power to send an undergraduate down, either permanently or for a limited period, to fine him and to gate him.

The Proctorial procession consists of two University policemen, the Proctor on duty and the University Marshal, who looks after the University Police and rings the bell at funerals; he is also responsible for the 17 lifebuoys on the river. The Proctors wear black velvet sleeved gowns and have the right to enter any public house or lodging house and also the right to challenge anybody to find out whether he or she is not a member of the University. They have no rights inside a college.

According to the rules undergraduates are forbidden to loiter in the streets, to form undesirable acquaintances or to march in procession through the streets. Leave has to be obtained to keep a car within 25 miles of Oxford, to fly or to hire a car, other than a taxi.

No theatrical performance may be given without the Vice-Chancellor's consent, and before undergraduates attend a non-University performance a certificate must be obtained from the Vice-Chancellor.

A list is published every term of approved hotels, restaurants, garages and dancing teachers.

I

Cap and gown are compulsory at all University ceremonies, sermons, lectures, examinations and out of college after hall at night. A white bow-tie has also to be worn by all men taking examinations. Women have to wear black stockings and black ties and no one is allowed to smoke in cap and gown.

In addition to the officers whom I have already mentioned there is a Public Orator, an Assistant-Registrar, a Secretary to the Curators of the Chest, a Secretary to the Board of the Faculties and two Burgesses, Sir Alan Herbert and Sir J. A. Salter.

There are three University Terms, the first, the Michaelmas Term, begins on or about the 13th of October; the second, the Hilary Term, begins in the second or third week of January and the third, the Trinity Term, begins in the last week in April. All the terms are of eight weeks' length leaving twenty-eight weeks of the year for vacation, during which the undergraduates are expected to do most of their reading.

The social life at Oxford is so busy that most undergraduates need long vacations in which to make up the leeway of reading for which they can find no time during term.

CHAPTER VIII

The Colleges

MEN

College	Date of foundation	Title of Head	Number of Undergraduates
All Souls	1438	Warden	None
Balliol	1282	Master	404
Brasenose	1509	Principal	390
Christ Church	1546	Dean	383
Corpus Christi	1516	President	148
Exeter	1314	Rector	302
Hertford	1284	Principal	171
Jesus	1571	President	226
Keble	1870	Warden	273
Lincoln	1427	Rector	250
Magdalen	1458	President	346
Merton	1264	Warden	229
New College	1379	Warden	385
Oriel	1326	Provost	255
Pembroke	1624	Master	156
Queen's	1340	Provost	315
*St Catherine's	1868	Censor	332
St Edmund Hall	1269	Principal	228
St John's	1555	President	251
St Peter's Hall	1928	Master	108
Trinity	1554	President	267
University	1249	Master	264
Wadham	1610	Warden	325
Worcester	1714	Provost	202

WOMEN

College	Date of foundation	Title of Head	Number of Undergraduates
Lady Margaret Hall	1878	Principal	256
*St Anne's	1879	Principal	303
St Hilda's	1893	Principal	211
St Hugh's	1886	Principal	203
Somerville	1879	Principal	276

*Non-residential

OTHER ESTABLISHMENTS

College	Date of foundation	Title of Head	Character
Campion Hall	1896	Dean	Catholic
Manchester	—	Principal	Non-denominational
Mansfield	1886	Principal	Congregationalist
Nuffield	1937	Warden	Social research
Pusey House	1884	Principal	Anglican
Ripon Hall	1898	Principal	C. of E. Theological College
Ruskin College	1899	Principal	Trades Union
St Benet's Hall	—	Master	Benedictine
St Stephen's House	1876	Principal	Theological College
Wycliffe Hall	1877	Principal	C. of E. Theological College

CHAPTER IX

Some Oxford Worthies

IT is not of course possible to deduce the character of a college from characters of its outstanding individual members, but it is fun trying to evolve for oneself the atmosphere and general outlook of a college from men whom one has known there and from the famous men of the past who have been attached to it. What is undeniable is the fact that colleges vary from one another in a very marked degree in their outlook, and what is perhaps even more important is the fact that each college changes its own character according to the personality of its head or outstanding dons.

The following list contains the names of some of those who have been connected with the different colleges and you may be left to work out for yourself which seems to be the college with which you would most like to be associated.

You will notice that the same famous name often occurs in connexion with more than one college. This only means that undergraduates of one college often become fellows of another, and all Regius Professors are attached to Christ Church, whatever their college.

Remember, too, that all members of All Souls are Fellows.

ALL SOULS:

Jeremy Taylor, Christopher Wren, Christopher Codrington, John Selden, Edward Young, A. L. Rowse, Lord Curzon, Lord Salisbury, Archbishop Lang, Sir William Blackstone, Thomas Linane, Reginald Heber, Lord Talbot, Thomas Linacre, Lord Simon, Lord Hugh Cecil, W. E. Gladstone.

BALLIOL:

John Wycliffe, Archbishop Temple, Cardinal Manning, Lord Peel, A. L. Smith, Robert Southey, Matthew Arnold, Arthur Hugh Clough, T. H. Green, Algernon Charles Swinburne, Herbert Asquith, Benjamin Jowett, Lord Curzon, Lord Milner, John Evelyn, S. C. Calverley, Andrew Lang, Lord Chief Justice Coleridge, Lord Lansdowne, Adam Smith, Archbishop Tait, J. E. Lockhart, Dr Baillie, Arnold Toynbee, Dr Caird, Earl Grey.

BRASENOSE:

John Foxe, Robert Burton, John Marston, Elias Ashmole, Reginald Heber, R. H. Barham, Walter Pater, John Buchan, Earl Haig, Dean Milman.

CHRIST CHURCH:

Cardinal Wolsey, Sir Philip Sidney, John Locke, Robert Burton, Richard Hakluyt, 'Lewis Carroll', W. E. Gladstone, John Ruskin, Canning, Chatham, Palmerston, Lord Salisbury, Edward VII, William Penn, John Wesley, Charles Wesley, Lord Rosebery, Lord Elgin, Dr Fell, Dean Liddell, Dean Aldrich, Dean Strong, Charles Boyle, George Grenville, Lord Mansfield, Lord Wellesley, Lord Liverpool, Sir Robert Peel, Dean Gaisford, Richard Corbet, Dean Colet, Sir Thomas More, John Lyly, Sir George Cornewall Lewis, Sidney Godolphin, Charles Wyndham, Carteret, Bolingbroke, Casaubon, Robert Hooke, Dr Pusey, Dr Liddon, Sir Peter Lely.

CORPUS CHRISTI:

Richard Hooker, John Jewel, General Oglethorpe, Richard Edgeworth, Thomas Day, Thomas Arnold, John Keble, John Ruskin.

EXETER:

Edward Burne-Jones, William Morris, J. A. Froude, F. D. Maurice, Sir John Eliot, Sir William Petre, William Strode, Earl of Shaftesbury, John Conant, Ray Lankester, William Sewell, John Ford, Sir Charles Lyall, R. D. Blackmore.

HERTFORD:

John Hobbes, Lord Clarendon, Sir Harry Vane, Sir Matthew Hale, Michael Drayton, Charles James Fox, Evelyn Waugh, John Selden, Henry Pelham, William Tyndale.

JESUS:

Henry Vaughan, T. E. Lawrence, J. R. Green, Beau Nash, Archbishop Usher, Sir Thomas Herbert, Sir Leoline Jenkins, James Howell.

KEBLE:

Lord Gladstone, Dr Winnington Ingram.

LINCOLN:

Sir William Davenant, Thomas Fuller, John Wesley, Robert Saunderson, Nathaniel Crewe, Dr Radcliffe, Mark Pattison, Lord Morley, Dr Merry.

MAGDALEN:

Cardinal Wolsey, Prince Rupert, Edward VIII, Joseph Addison, Edmund Gibbon, Oscar Wilde, Compton Mackenzie, William Collins, Edmund Cartwright, Stephen Hawker, C. S. Lewis, Henry Sacheverell, Dr Routh, Lord Selbourne, Bishop Hough, George Wither.

MERTON:

John Wycliffe, Andrew Irvine, Duns Scotus, Edmund Blunden, Bishop Jewel, Bishop Hooper, Sir Thomas Bodley, William Harvey, Anthony Wood, Lord Randolph Churchill, Lord Halsbury, Sir Henry Savile, Bishop Rede, Dr Mandel Creighton.

NEW COLLEGE:

William Spooner, Archbishop Chichele, William Grocyn, Sir Henry Wotton, Bishop Ken, Judge Holloway, Bishop Lowth, Sydney Smith, Lord Milner, William Waynflete, Captain John White, John Galsworthy, H. A. L. Fisher.

ORIEL:

Sir Walter Raleigh, Gilbert White, Newman, Matthew Arnold, Samuel Wilberforce, Keble, Tom Hughes, Sir Thomas More, Cecil Rhodes, John Barclay, Bishop Butler, Edward Talbot, Lord Goschen, Doctor John Hunter, William Prynne, Edward Pusey, John Hampden, Lord Morley.

PEMBROKE:

Thomas Heywood, Francis Beaumont, John Pym, Sir Thomas Browne, Dr Johnson, George Whitefield, William Shenstone, William Blackstone, Dr Birkbeck Hill, G. W. Steevens, Bishop Mitchinson.

QUEEN'S:

William Temple, Joseph Addison, Wycherley, Jeremy Bentham, Francis Jeffrey, A. H. Sayce, John Wycliffe, the Black Prince, Henry V, Leonard Digges.

ST EDMUND HALL:

Sir John Stainer, Dr George Bate, Thomas Hearne, Dr Moore.

JOHN'S:

Archbishop Laud, Archbishop Juxon, Archbishop Chichele, John Shirley, Dr Wheatley, Abraham Tucker.

TRINITY:

James Harrington, Archbishop Sheldon, Henry Crashaw, Ludlow, John Evelyn, Lord North, Thomas Warton, Richard Burton, Newman, William Stubbs, E. A. Freeman, Walter Savage Landor (sent down), W. G. Palgrave, Sir John Denham, William Chillingworth, Colonel Ireton, John Aubrey, Dr Bathurst, William Pitt, Lord Chatham, Lord Selborne, Sir Arthur Quiller-Couch.

UNIVERSITY:

Percy Bysshe Shelley (sent down), Lord Stowell, Lord Eldon, Edmund Ludlow, Dean Stanley, Goldwin Smith, Sir Edwin Arnold, Earl of Rochester, Lord Somers, Doctor John Radcliffe, Lord Herbert of Cherbury, John Aubrey.

WADHAM:

Christopher Wren, C. B. Fry, Lord Birkenhead, Lord Simon, Robert Blake, John Wilkins, Speaker Onslow, Lord Westbury, Sir T. G. Jackson.

WORCESTER:

Richard Lovelace, Thomas de Quincey, Sir Kenelm Digby, Sir William Clarke.

CHAPTER X

Odds and Ends

NOTICE AT ENTRANCE TO CHRIST CHURCH MEADOWS

'The Meadow keepers and Constables are hereby instructed to prevent the entrance into the Meadow of all beggars, all persons in ragged or very dirty clothes, persons of improper character or who are not decent in appearance and behaviour: to prevent indecent, rude, or disorderly conduct of any description.

To allow no handcarts, wheelbarrows, bath-chairs or perambulators (unless they have had previous permission from the Very Reverend the Dean) and no hawkers or persons carrying parcels or bundles so as to obstruct the walks.

To prevent the flying of kites, throwing stones, throwing balls, bowling hoops, shooting arrows, firing guns or pistols, or playing games attended with danger or inconvenience to passers-by: also fishing in the waters, catching birds, or bird-nesting.'

SOME UNIVERSITY RULES TAKEN FROM THE LAUDIAN STATUTES

1. They shall be obliged to abstain from that absurd and assuming practice of walking publicly in boots.

2. They are not to encourage the growth of curls, or immoderately long hair.

3. Scholars of all conditions shall keep away from inns, eating-houses, wine-shops – if any person does otherwise, and is not 18 years old, and not a graduate, he shall be flogged in public.

4. All scholars shall retire before nine o'clock to their proper colleges and halls.

5. They must refrain from every kind of sport or exercise, whence danger, wrong, or inconvenience may arise to others, from hunting wild animals (fallow deer, hares and rabbits for instance) with hounds of any kind, ferrets, nets or toils.

6. Neither rope-dancers nor players are to be permitted within the University of Oxford – All stage-players transgressors are to be incarcerated.

7. No scholars are to play football within the University or its precinct whether alone by themselves, or in company with townsmen – nor are they to appear as lookers-on at such pastimes.

8. No member of a hall shall speak any other language than Latin on any occasion within the ambit of the hall except to illiterates and strangers.

9. Everyone who is going for a walk into the town or country is to take a companion with him as a witness of his conduct under pain of a penny.

10.   No one shall keep or fondle dogs for hunting or of any other kind or hawks within the orbit of the hall.

11.   No one shall prevent his fellows from studying or sleeping by singing, making a noise, shouting or discharging a gun.

12.   At Christ Church Junior Students will leave their surplices unbuttoned in front to prevent hunting pink being worn underneath.

S. C. CALVERLEY AT A 'VIVA'

EXAMINER   And with what feelings ought we to regard the decalogue?

CALVERLEY   (Who had no idea what the decalogue was) With feelings of devotion, mingled with awe.

EXAMINER   Quite right, young man, a very proper answer.

T. E. LAWRENCE EXPLORES A SEWER

'He had brought a candle to stick in the bows of the canoe, and an acetylene cycle lamp at the stern. As we drifted down the darkness of the sewer, he remarked casually that it would be interesting to notice, as the foulness of the air increased, which light would be extinguished first, and what the attitude of rats might be. "At any rate", he added as we lay prone in the canoe, "there is no room to turn back." But Folly Bridge was reached in under twenty minutes – the trip became quite popular until it was stopped by authority.'

Canon E. F. HALL

THE AUTHOR OF THE *Anatomy of Melancholy* RELAXES

Whenever he fell into despondency he could only get relief by going to the bridge-foot at Oxford and hearing the barge-men swear at one another, at which he would set his hands to his sides and laugh profanely.

BISHOP KENNET ON ROBERT BURTON

ANOTHER FAMOUS MELANCHOLIC RELAXES

JOHNSON   The first day after I came to college I waited upon my tutor, and then stayed away four. On the sixth, he asked me why I had not attended. I told him that I had been sliding in Christ Church Meadow. I had no notion that I was wrong or irreverent to my tutor.

BOSWELL   That, sir, was great fortitude of mind.

JOHNSON   No, sir: stark insensibility.

A VISITING JOURNALIST RELAXES

Stanley Parker hadn't a girl friend to take to Christ Church Commemoration Ball, social event of the year at Oxford University, so he took a chair instead. He set it down, bought it a drink, and waited for the fun to start.

It was a good idea. In no time half the girls present wanted to dance with the lonely man, and the chair came in useful for their partners to sit on. And this is how Stanley finally finished – with Smokey Reaves, 23, an American student at the University, as his partner for the evening.

Caption to a photograph of a man holding in his arms a girl in a chair in the Daily Mirror *July 1st,* 1948.

A POET-BISHOP RELAXES

After Richard Corbet was Doctor of Divinity he sang Ballads at the Cross at Abingdon on a market-day. He was made Dean of Christ Church and Bishop of Oxford. His Chaplain, Dr Lushington was a very learned and ingenious man; and they loved one another. The Bishop would take the key of the wine cellar, and he and his Chaplain would go and lock themselves in and be merry. Then first he lays down his Episcopal hat – 'There lies the Doctor'. Then he puts off his gown – 'There lies the Bishop'. Then turns – 'Here's to thee, Corbet', 'Here's to thee, Lushington'.

JOHN AUBREY

A FUTURE POET LAUREATE REFUSES TO RELAX

As an undergraduate Robert Bridges was a notable oarsman, and he was probably the only man who ever refused to stroke the Oxford University boat. This he did on the ground that he could not spare time from the work which he was then doing for his medical degree.

OXFORD MAIL on BRIDGES

A FELLOW DAMNED IN A FAIR WIFE

Richard Hooker, fellow of Corpus Christi, was very unhappy in a wife who would make him rock the cradle purposely to hinder his study but whilst he did that office with one hand he would hold the book in the other. She would not allow him paper to write upon. She afterwards married a captain who turned Hooker's children out of doors, so that in a short time they either begged their bread or died in the streets with hunger.

ANTHONY À WOOD

Epilogue

'KNOW YE her secret none can utter?' asked Sir Arthur Quiller Couch of Trinity.

'Know you the secret none discover?
Tell it – when you go down'

I have been down over forty years and if I am ever to tell it I must tell it now. How can I when it is not discoverable?

I could as soon attempt to tell you the secret of the hills. All hillmen agree that the hills have a secret. All Oxford men agree that Oxford has a secret. I would willingly unveil it for you if I could. All I can do is to pull off palimpsest after palimpsest and hope that you will be enabled to enjoy one-tenth part of the happiness that Oxford has given me.

When I think quickly of the word Oxford, what images are formed in my mind? A very confused medley indeed.

I see an unpopular undergraduate, unpopular because he dared to proclaim that he was a theosophist, being debagged and thrown into the icy waters of Mercury in Peckwater Quad, Christ Church at midnight in the snow of mid-February.

I see Bill Milligan, Olympic miler racing four times round this same quadrangle while Lord Birkenhead races round once. This contest decided on the top of a riotous and rich dinner in Hall resulted in a dead heat.

I see the Grand Stand erected on the Christ Church ground for the Oxford Pageant being set on fire by Members of the House to celebrate their success on the river in Eights and those incendiaries retreating post haste into the black waters of the Cher as the result of the Fire Brigade hose being deviated from the fire to the setters-on-fire.

I see an extremely attractive crowd of undergraduates bescarfed but hatless accompanied by even more attractive girls in New Look skirts and shining hair entering and leaving the King's Arms at noon on a sunny November Saturday.

I see slightly longer-haired men and shorter-haired young women queueing up for luncheon at the Kemp Cafeteria.

I see a procession of white-tied harassed young men and black stockinged even more harassed young women cycling towards the Examination Schools.

I see burly young men in scarcely any clothes at all swinging down the Broad Walk of Christ Church Meadows towards the College Barges gaily

85

decorated with bunting, geraniums and College flags during Eights Week.

I see young couples immaculately dressed sitting out under the light of a midsummer moon in the dark shadows of the wall of the Canon's garden during a Christ Church Commemoration Ball.

I see earnest, undergrown, under-nourished, spotty-faced, bespectacled youths wearing all the cares of the world on their perplexed faces poring over esoteric text books in the Radcliffe Camera.

I see the Master of the Christ Church Beagles all verdant green above and spotless white below leading his score of ardent followers into the horse-brake which stands at Canterbury Gate.

I hear the crack of the riding whip and the hunting cries of the too wealthy, too unintelligent, but extremely gregarious Billingdon or Rousers in Canterbury Quad waiting to go off to ride to hounds with the Bicester or the Heythrop.

I watch with misgiving and listen with distaste to the exhibitionists of both sexes who wear magenta trousers, yellow polo-jerseys and unkempt lengthy locks and talk as if to be heard across Niagara when their voices really only have to carry across the Randolph bar.

Camp-followers and vivandieres of the dramatic and other arts are to be found, of course, in Chelsea and Bloomsbury. Like madness in England it isn't really noticeable there, but in Oxford the atmosphere is apt to be chilly for the bogus.

I see inspired lecturers, Sir Walter Raleigh, his hands trembling so much that he can scarcely hold his notes, Lord David Cecil, his hands being wrung out like Macbeth's after the murder of Duncan, C. S. Lewis, portly and agate-like, drawing seraph-like looks of devotion from serried rows of earnest young women who find him 'too, too adorable', and not always too easy to report verbatim.

I hear swaying crowds packed in the stands of the Iffley Road Rugger ground roar 'Come on Oxford' as the University forwards burst through the opposing scrum and take the ball down the field.

I see under a hot June sun the stately procession of famous men whom Oxford delights to honour, clad in the crimson silk of the newly acquired Doctor's gown passing from the Sheldonian Theatre into the blaze of the outer air.

I see the silhouettes of fair women and gay young men moving to and fro in the upper windows of rooms in Peckwater as Great Tom booms out the hour of five minutes past nine.

I see girls in incredibly short shorts or most becoming bathing dresses punting with skill and grace and full knowledge of the attention which they draw both from the bank and the eyes of the reclining swain who lies full length at his ease in the bottom of the boat.

I watch with less pleasure the muscular forms of the sports-loving ladies of Lady Margaret Hall, swimming strongly and breathing noisily as they race to catch up with the retreating canoe.

I watch with no pleasure at all other sports-loving ladies clad most hideously and bulging in the oddest places racing up and down the Parks with hockey sticks, silent maenads.

I fight my way to the fore among the browsers among the books at Blackwalls, and among the supporters of the bar at the King's Arms.

I sit surrounded by the very great (athletically) in Vincent's and am both charmed and disarmed by their complete normality and their most becoming modesty. It is the rarest thing in Oxford to see a Blue wearing his Blue. You can nearly always distinguish a Blue from other men by his sub-fusc ties and subdued tones of dress. He is the one quite inconspicuous type of undergraduate. He is usually working. The fact that he has to work at his play means that he works at his work. He even eats like a workman. It is not for him to dally with the tangles of Neaera's hair in the Kemp or settle down to a lengthy discussion of Stravinsky in the bar at White's. He scorns delights, he lives laborious days. Fame, however, whether he likes it or not, fame (that last infirmity of noble minds) is his, such fame that even forty years afterwards the most unlikely people still remember his initials. Perhaps it is lucky that all super-athletes, except W. G. Grace and C. B. Fry, were blessed at their christening with three Christian names. Three initials are so much easier to remember than two.

What does Oxford mean to me now that I am coming to the end of my life?

It means the exquisite delight of lying in the sun in the silence of St John's gardens, with only the blue sky above, grey walls all round and a wealth of trees and flowers by my side. It means the society of youth, and nothing gives me greater pleasure than the companionship of adolescents of both sexes. They not only help to keep me young in spirit, they keep me intellectually alert.

Most of all Oxford in spite of all that has happened to her and is daily happening to her steadily and surely maintains a definite continuity. Something of the Oxford of the Middle Ages, surely the best of it, survives.

If it is, as Matthew Arnold assumed, the home of lost causes, that is a matter for pride and congratulation, for most lost causes are good causes, not least the cause of freedom and individuality and enterprise which the present régime are fighting so hard to destroy.